CW00469256

# BFI TV Classics

BFI TV Classics is a series of books celebrating key individual television programmes and series. Television scholars, critics and novelists provide critical readings underpinned with careful research, alongside a personal response to the programme and a case for its 'classic' status.

**Also Published:**

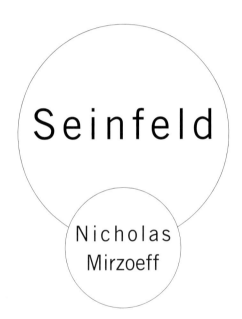

# Seinfeld

## Nicholas Mirzoeff

First published in 2007 by the
**British Film Institute**
21 Stephen Street, London W1T 1LN

The British Film Institute's purpose is to champion moving image culture in all its richness and diversity across the UK, for the benefiit of as wide an audience as possible, and to create and encourage debate.

Images from *Seinfeld*, West-Shapiro Productions/Castle Rock Entertainment.

British Library Cataloguing-in-Publication Data
A catalogue record for this book is available from the British Library

ISBN 978-1-84457-201-4

Set by D R Bungay Associates, Burghfiield, Berkshire

Printed in the UK by The Cromwell Press, Trowbridge, Wiltshire

# Contents

# 1 One Man and His TV

Los Angeles, 1990. I place a box of rare, mostly American records on the orange shag-pile carpet of my new rental apartment. The fake Tudor beams of the living room are an interesting counterpoint to the equally fake shiny white plaster classical statues in the lobby, sitting on their bright green fake grass. In the swirl of cultural signals, I think I know what to do. I turn on the TV, using the manual dial on the small colour set. Before long, I am comfortably at home in *Cheers*, *Taxi* and *Soap*. Venturing into unknown territory, I am soon pleased to discover a radical new form of American comedy. This mock-documentary took an utterly dead-pan approach to its material, the style later made famous by Steve Coogan's character Alan Partridge, as if it really cared about its subject, with only the absurdist title giving the game away. *Lifestyles of the Rich and Famous*. Genius. Once I made some friends, I quickly told them about this brilliant format only to be told, of course, that it was not a comedy but a purportedly serious programme. Is irony in the eye of the beholder? Not entirely. Once I knew what it was, *Lifestyles* lost its magic for me. It was clear I didn't know my way around. I needed a guide to what was funny in America. Beginning in that autumn of 1990, a comedy that was at first called *The Seinfeld Chronicles* and then simply *Seinfeld* was that guide. *Seinfeld* taught America a new way to be funny. It also taught me, and I suspect many others, how to be American. American of a certain sort, that is, one that Europeans suspect does not even exist. An ironic, even sardonic place, mostly Jewish, also queer, with issues about race and gender.

With *Seinfeld*, I moved to New York, a New York of the mind to which the real place, where I now live, sometimes matches up, sometimes not. Many Americans live in the New York of the mind. Usually arts and humanities graduates, they live where they can or where they have to for professional or personal reasons but take home delivery of the *New York Times* and the *New Yorker*, have a local coffee place to go to and once made sure to see the latest Woody Allen movie. Now they watch the *Seinfeld* rerun at 11. The New York of sophistication, imagination and sexual liberation that is being conjured up in all this performance does not really exist, even in New York. So *Seinfeld* imagines its characters in a variety of styles and ways of acting in a dream New York that everyone of a certain sort wants to inhabit. Today people take the Kramer Reality Tour or visit the coffee shop in *Seinfeld* on Broadway and 112th Street in search of that New York, just as they might take a trip to Greenwich Village, where the beatniks have long been replaced by real-estate moguls, or

2

The *Seinfeld* diner

to SoHo, where the artists' loft spaces have been converted into high-street shopping chains.

This is a book about watching *Seinfeld* in that time and place, which has become the 1990s, epitomised by the Clinton presidency and *Seinfeld* itself. As I am not a media studies specialist, I have not followed the usual rules in regards to the critical analysis of television. My model here is the French literary critic Roland Barthes. When Barthes came to write about photography, he decided that, given his lack of technical knowledge, he could only take the position of the viewer, rather than that of the photographer.[1] So this book is not based on interviews with the stars or the writers, or some other form of inside information. I have found in writing on contemporary art that as soon as I make the acquaintance of an artist, it changes the way I can write about them. In a subtle way, you find yourself wanting to support the artist and draw back from criticism for fear of giving offence to your new friend. Television and film now make active efforts to make viewers feel part of this backstage environment, supplying all manner of detail on DVD extras and in print or television journalism. Knowing only too well how crucial fan cultures are to the survival of a television series, programme-makers have actively cultivated them since the success of Chris Carter's fan-friendly cult series *The X Files* (1993–2002). Somehow, this strategy doesn't seem right for a show that clearly subscribed to Groucho Marx's reservation that he did not want to be a member of any club that would take him. It would be difficult to follow *Seinfeld*'s narrative and character development, as there was no consistent, overarching storyline within individual seasons (with the exception of the fourth series, which is discussed in the next chapter), let alone the entire series. Of course, individual episodes were very tightly written but there is no deadlier form of writing than the lengthy explanation of other people's comedy that tends towards the inevitable word-for-word recitation associated with *Monty Python* (1969–74) fans of a certain sort. By the same token, *Seinfeld* characters were instrumental to a given plot need. As the *Seinfeld* writer Larry Charles once put it, the characters do not learn from experience and remain who they are.

3

To take just one example, the character of George Costanza was played from the first by Jason Alexander as a Woody Allen pastiche, with the strong implication that he was therefore Jewish. But in the seventh series, the plot of one episode hinges on George's father, Frank, returning to his native Italy to find his long-lost cousin in the village of Costanza (episode 127, 'The Doll', 1996). No consequence ever ensued for any of the Costanza characters from this 'revelation'.

So, like *Seinfeld*, this book takes pleasure in being digressive and discursive in the pursuit of amusement, taking the show to represent a cultural phenomenon emblematic of its period, and thereby a classic, rather than as a self-contained work of art. It is a book about watching television, based on the experience of watching *Seinfeld* over and over in first run, repeats, syndication (when the original broadcaster licenses the show to other channels for endless reruns) and finally on DVD. I want to ask what I thought I was doing watching the same programmes over and over again, knowing all the jokes but still finding it funny. What's up with funny anyway? Why is it so important to be funny, especially if you're Jewish like Groucho Marx, Woody Allen, Lenny Bruce, Sid Caesar, Jack Benny, Jackie Mason and so on and on? Did I learn to be American-Jewish for the jokes, like Tim Whatley (Bryan Cranston) the convert dentist in *Seinfeld* (episode 153, 'The Yada Yada', 1997)?

It might seem a stretch to take television as a guide to reality, let alone situation comedy (sitcom), among the most critically despised but also among the most watched of scripted formats, with due allowance for the still 'lower' genres of chat shows, reality TV and so on. It might even be that sitcom has become more fondly thought of now that *Big Brother* (1999–) and its ilk dominate the airwaves. Let's say right away that television is not the way to make major life choices. But it influences people in many smaller ways, some of which we admit to, some of which we deny or repress. For instance, thousands of women had a 'Rachel haircut' in the early 1990s, meaning a style like that worn by the actress Jennifer Aniston who plays the character Rachel Green in the sitcom *Friends* (1994–2004). *Seinfeld* itself launched a variety of catchphrases into everyday American usage, such as 'yada yada', 'not

that there's anything wrong with that' and 'master of my domain'.
Again and again, the cast insisted in interviews that the characters were
not to be taken as role models. In a debate as to which member of a
recently defunct relationship should not attend a party to which both
are invited, Jerry took the view that George should go and his former
girlfriend should stay away out of politeness. However, Elaine feels the
woman should go because she was the winner and, as she says, 'To the
victor the spoils!' (episode 70, 'The Lip Reader', 1993). The answer is
ridiculous and so it's funny. It was not meant to be used by people in this
kind of situation, but rather to acknowledge that such morally and
emotionally confusing moments do occur in contemporary life, and
perhaps to make you feel better about it by laughing.

Television insinuates itself into our lives in such ways and is a
significant part of most people's lives in itself. Someone has to be
watching for all those hours that a television is on in the average
household (somewhere between four and six, depending on whom you
believe). As the digital boosters of the 1990s had it, television was our
first experience of virtual reality. By this they meant that we don't
simply watch television in the passive way designated by the term 'couch
potato' but imagine ourselves in and as part of television. Now that
people of all ages are sophisticated viewers of the medium, television has
moved beyond a simple aspiration to be a given character or to be with
that character. It both comments on and creates the 'rules' of everyday
life, providing a collective reference point for individual action in a new
and confusing media-dominated society simply by being funny about it.
This was a period in which a dating guide called *The Rules* stipulated
the tactics of 'playing hard to get', such as the strategy that women
should not call men and rarely return their calls. Ellen Fein and Sherrie
Shamoon, the authors, declared that 'Nineties women simply have not
been schooled in the basics!'[2] This book was aimed at women who
wanted a guide to getting married. By the same token, you could learn
how to be funny from *Seinfeld*, and how Americans in general had tried
to be funny, no small thing for an immigrant, especially a person like
myself who relies on humour to negotiate social situations. My edgy

5

British self-deprecation and sarcasm were received with baffled incomprehension and I retooled myself using *Seinfeld* as a database. It worked. This book examines how *Seinfeld* made and reflected the 'rules', first for humour itself and then for the related questions of ethnicity, religion and sexuality – what else are jokes about?

Watching *Seinfeld* was visually easy and verbally complex. The camera placed you in the circle of friends as an extra participant, never looking down on them (literally or metaphorically) or up, as from the point of view of a child, unless the script called for it. The very neutrality of its design and camerawork (what a film director would call the *mise en scène*, placing in a scene) helped make the viewer feel part of *Seinfeld*'s world. In a period in which network television began to experiment with such devices as the jump-cut in drama series like *NYPD Blue* (1993–2005), *Seinfeld* taxed its viewers' intellectual resources but not their visual sense. Jerry Seinfeld insisted that the show be made using film, rather than the cheaper videotape, because it gives a far more realistic feel, as one look at the current digital format in use for American daytime soaps like *All My Children* (1970–) makes clear. Film gives more depth, better colour and detail and a more even sense of light than video but is much more expensive to use and edit. At the same time, *Seinfeld*'s verbal complexity generated seventy-page scripts for each episode, more than twenty pages longer than the average sitcom. Despite all this verbiage, *Seinfeld*'s verbal and physical comedy relied on its audience making a series of associations and connections, not all of which were spelled out by the text. Making those connections was part of the pleasure of watching the programme. It was fascinated by everyday life and the small choices and frustrations it involves, like dry-clean-only clothes, fat-free food and the formatting of personal organisers. These consumer items were all new at the time and came haunted with anxieties. Is 'dry-clean only' really true or a deal for dry cleaners? Is 'fat-free' the same as good for you? And how is a personal organiser going to make you more organised if you can't make the thing work?

One of the particular intricacies of Jerry Seinfeld's comedy was that he endlessly discussed sex and sexuality without using explicit

language. Unlike many stand-up comedians who have one act for
television and another, more explicit one for live performance, Seinfeld's
act was the same on and off the air. Likewise, a key part of *Seinfeld*'s
humour relied on the viewer to complete the 'get', meaning that the
subject under discussion was alluded to rather than directly described.
This referential style allowed the sexual subject matter so typical of
what was then called alternative comedy to transfer to mainstream
television, precisely because it was not directly named. The audience
were at once amused and pleased with themselves for making the 'get'.
So this book will not fall into the pedantic trap of spelling out exactly
what form of sexual activity *Seinfeld* refers to in its depictions of 1990s'
New York, relying on its readers to enjoy the not overly taxing task of
decoding. Much of the show's overt content also detailed the analysis of
verbal and physical signs. Does leaving an exercise machine without
wiping the sweat off constitute a form of physical intimacy? Where
exactly was the stress placed in a sentence? The characters often seem
lost in their own world, as if stranded in the 1990s without a guide, and
yet hypercritical and hyperconscious of all that went on around them.
One whole genre of advertising of the period relied on just such a
double-bind. The soft drink Sprite began promoting itself in the 1990s
using the slogan 'Image is Nothing. Thirst is Everything'. The ad itself
told you to despise ads, while selling you a drink that because of its high
sugar content would do nothing at all for whatever thirst you might
have had. Advertisers began to sell us not only products but a sense that
we are too clever to be influenced by their crude blandishments, even as
the mass out there somewhere succumbs. If comedy is a form of sales
pitch for the comedian, *Seinfeld* was an extremely successful variant,
as evidenced by the remarkably high rates charged by the National
Broadcasting Company (NBC) for advertising slots during the show.
If you make a Google search for *Seinfeld*, most of the results that come
up are very dry articles referring to the success of the show as a vehicle
for advertising.

One indication of *Seinfeld*'s significance as a guide to its time is
the reliance on the 'get' as a political device of the period. When Bill

Clinton was a candidate for President, his manner was such that he managed to sell two different perceptions of himself to Americans. Some conservative-leaning people were convinced that he was really one of them by his Southern accent, Christian references and his symbolic attack on the African-American performer Sister Souljah. Liberals were equally convinced that he was simply playing this part to engineer an electoral victory, relying on cues such as his apparently liberal wife Hillary, his avoidance of the draft during the Vietnam War and his sheer intelligence. Like a comedian, Clinton would exit his campaign performances on a great line, 'I still believe in a place called Hope', which can mean whatever you want it to mean. A number of *Seinfeld* shows attempted this exit but only a few really worked. One of the best was the actress Teri Hatcher's declaration about her breasts, after a show dedicated to the question of whether they had been enhanced: 'They're real and they're spectacular' (episode 59, 'The Implant', 1993).

'They're real and they're spectacular'

Clinton also found that it was not so easy to live up to the double-bind he had put himself into in order to get elected. By making his statement on gays in the military, he at once and permanently enraged his conservative voters, who realised that they had been had and could not wait to pay him back in the Congressional elections of 1994 that delivered a Republican majority that has lasted for twelve years at the time of writing. Nonetheless, Clinton was able to achieve enough of a 'get' to push through measures like the North American Free Trade Agreement and welfare cutbacks that his own Democratic Party often disagreed with. This reliance on the 'get' as a strategy did not make *Seinfeld* in and of itself conservative or liberal. The show avoided the political dramas of the day, even when the farcical impeachment of Clinton with its obsession with whether a presidentially soiled blue dress had been dry-cleaned seemed to be re-enacting its own obsessions. As a show about New York Jews, its liberal/Democratic position was assumed but not directly stated.

No television format was more vital to the American networks in the 1990s than the sitcom. When the British cultural studies critic Raymond Williams visited America in the 1970s, he saw at once that television there depended on 'flow'.[3] That is to say, the goal of the network is to keep the viewer watching, as programmes change and are interrupted by advertisements, without changing channel, losing attention or even switching off. With the emergence of cable television generating more alternatives and the development of the remote control making channel switching even easier, television planners in the 1990s stepped up their efforts. For NBC, the strategy revolved around the notion of 'Must See TV'. The plan was that the viewer would stay with NBC because its shows (executive-speak for programmes) were essential viewing. In order to seem culturally of the moment, hip and with it, a person needed to see these shows and have something to say about them. The format centred around Thursday night, the lead into the weekend when the advertiser-desired demographic of 18–34-year-olds was presumed to be out and not watching TV. The hope was that they would be talking about what they had seen on Thursday. The system was simple at heart: after the early evening combination of local and national news, followed by game shows and trash TV delights like *Access Hollywood* (1996–), a gossip and celebrities vehicle, the line-up proper began at 8pm. Four 'half-hour' (twenty-two minutes of programme in a thirty-minute slot) comedies would lead in to the 'serious' hour-long (forty-four minutes of programme in a sixty-minute slot) legal or hospital drama at 10pm, thereby delivering a substantial audience to local affiliates' 11pm local news. All of this serious money came to hinge around a show 'about nothing', as discussed in the next chapter.

It worked so well because a generation whose attention was devoutly sought by advertisers, the legendary 18–34 age group, who spend most of their money on consumer goods, watched *Seinfeld* in disproportionate numbers. While series like the earnest *thirtysomething* (1987–91) had made the careers and families of a group of college friends the centre of drama, *Seinfeld* took a similar group and made it the subject of comedy. The series centred on the apartment life of the comedian Jerry Seinfeld, whose character is that of the comedian of the same name who plays himself. With his passion for eating cereal and obsessive neatness, Seinfeld seemed like a real character precisely because he was one. Any lead needs a sidekick and George Costanza, was the perfect Sancho Panza, even if Seinfeld himself was not quite Don Quixote. George was based on the insecurities and preoccupations of the producer Larry David, who was a comedian himself and has gone on to further success with *Curb Your Enthusiasm* (2000–), a *Seinfeld* without the euphemisms. The character of Kramer, Jerry's neighbour, was based on the real-life Kenny Kramer, who had lived next door to Larry David in New York. Of all the characters in the show, Kramer, played by Michael Richards, became the one that most epitomised its unusual take on life, attested to by the presence of the 'Kramer Reality Tour' of New York and Kramer T-shirts in tourist-oriented gift shops today. The ensemble was completed by Elaine, played by Julia Louis-Dreyfus, an ex-girlfriend of Jerry's, an unusual situation for a woman character. Although Elaine served as a point of reference for the

10

The four *Seinfeld* main characters

Jerry Seinfeld as 'Jerry Seinfeld'

George Costanza (Jason Alexander)

Elaine Benes (Julia Louis Dreyfus)

Cosmo Kramer (Michael Richards)

masculine preoccupations of the others, she was anything but the lovable-girl-next-door type usually cast in such roles. Her physical aggressiveness, expressive face and lacerating wit made her more than a match for her companions.

The four characters represented four different takes on the possible careers and lives of young-ish people at the time, people who had been to college, tried a couple of career options, had a few relationships, maybe one serious, but were still unsettled about where things were going to end up. If this biographical approach seems a surprising take on the show about nothing, notice that the second category of clips in the 100th show special, after 'relationships', was 'ambitions', mostly unfulfilled needless to say. The main characters are all in their early thirties as the series begins and age only very gradually as it goes on. Seinfeld has the cool career – in this case, comedian – that many liberal arts or humanities graduates aspire to, perhaps even make some steps towards, but rarely achieve. George is more typical of most of us: a college graduate, but working as a real-estate agent, not at all the career he wants. When he gets fired, he says to his parents, who want him to settle for the civil service (a less privileged position in the US than it would be in the UK): 'I do know that I have some kind of a talent – something to offer. I just don't know what it is yet!' (episode 66, 'The Puffy Shirt', 1993). For one glorious episode, George gets to be a hand model, effortlessly earning money and attracting women, until he disparages a puffy shirt, causing its designer to push him so that he thrusts his hands onto a hot iron. For the Georges of this world, a glimpse of happiness is just a chance to achieve even greater failure. Elaine, like many young women, has made her 'chosen field' publishing. Her career is not easy, with false starts and setbacks but, even though she seems to change places with George for one frightening episode (episode 86, 'The Opposite', 1994), she finds a place writing for the J. Peterman catalogue, which may not have the literary cachet of her earlier hopes of working for renowned presses like Doubleday or Knopf, but is a salaried position with benefits, albeit at the mercy of her eccentric boss J. Peterman. Kramer represents the bohemian dream,

13

Elaine in publishing – almost

14

Elaine realises she has become George

living the urban life without a paying job and yet never falling into poverty. Always running a scheme or a scam, Kramer has no greater good in mind than his own advancement, even if this is limited to a free box of Cuban cigars or a cut on some second-hand raincoats. The focus on aspirations makes it clear why *Seinfeld* sometimes seems to be more about George than Jerry – when I first saw it, I assumed George was the lead character. Many aspirations that are generated in early life go unfulfilled, or so it often seems, and many conversations between people in their thirties can be summarised as discussions about 'settling', whether for jobs, houses or partners that seem less than ideal.

The primary venues in the series for these more or less realistic middle-class career choices are Jerry's rent-controlled one-bedroom apartment on the Upper West Side of New York, a feasible place for a thirty-something to be living at the time. The walls are drab and the furniture unremarkable, as one would expect. The lighting in the early series often muted the scene, rather than providing the brightly coloured, larger-than-life environment of the standard sitcom. Both of these choices were deliberately parodied in *Jerry*, the show-within-the-show, sold to NBC by Jerry and George. In their pilot for the series that was never to be made, the character Jerry lives in a large, over-furnished apartment that is brightly decorated and lit (episode 64, 'The Pilot, part 2', 1993). The action that may take place elsewhere is then always digested and analysed at Monk's coffee shop, a cheap full-service restaurant of the traditional New York kind that is now gradually disappearing. These locations came to dominate the show as it developed, making the other scenes incidental to the analysis and discussion in the apartment and the coffee shop. As often happens to college-educated strivers with connections to wealthier or more successful friends, moments of the New York good life are dangled in front of the group, such as tickets to expensive sport games or the opera, visits to country houses and cabins, or first-class travel. Before long these glimpses of the 'bright lights, shining city' world of New York celebrity and prosperity are snatched away from our unfabulous four, who find themselves again arguing over the remote in the apartment or

15

The *Seinfeld* apartment

The apartment in *Jerry*

back at Monk's for yet another cup of coffee. Their routine failure to excel reassured their viewers either that it was OK for them to not yet be doing as well as they might like – or conversely that their place was better than it might otherwise seem. At the same time, under the guise of comedy, it addressed the nameless and unnameable fear of the American middle-class that life amounts to nothing. Is nothing funny? What are the rules for a life that is nothing? Is being nothing good for the Jews? How do you date if there's nothing at stake? It's all 'about nothing', and that can be an idea for a show …

This book takes the life about nothing as seen on TV as its subject. In the chapters that follow, I first ask what it was to make a television series about nothing in the 1990s. *Seinfeld* had to come to terms with itself as a television programme, rather than a play or literary product. When it did so, it abandoned the formal concept of having no subject, while maintaining its insistence on 'no hugging, no learning'. *Seinfeld* pursued its obsession with the rules of social behaviour as its only consistent theme. In the next chapter, I look at how *Seinfeld* made comedy from the stuff of everyday life in New York, with its permanent array of irritations, centred around the suspicion that another person might think they're better than you. This comedy of spite also harboured a certain egalitarianism, raising the ultimate forbidden question in American life of class difference. As the 1990s progressed, New York became divided by wealth as never before, so that Manhattan has become an island dominated by privilege. While such questions are hinted at in *Seinfeld*, they are dealt with by displacement into the key comedy categories of ethnicity and sexuality. In *Seinfeld*, the ethnicity in question is Jewish in a period when the Oslo Peace Accord seemed to be on the verge of redefining Jewishness by means of solving the Middle East issue. In the chapter 'Too Jewish?', I suggest that Jerry Seinfeld represented a new form of Jewishness, willing to joke about anti-Semitism and circumcision, while being very much part of the tradition of Jewish humour from Yiddish theatre to Jack Benny and Woody Allen. At the centre of this humour is the question of sex and sexuality, the subject of the next chapter. Here more than anywhere else the

17

characters are lost, knowing what they are not supposed to do more clearly than what they should and chronically uncertain about what, and indeed who, they actually want. George worries that he might be gay, Jerry is perceived as gay, George and Jerry are outed as a gay couple and Elaine seeks to convert a gay man to her team. With Elaine's character acting very much like one of the guys, the concern here was the boundary between male friendship and same-sex desire that made great comic play with the post-Stonewall uncertainties of dating life in New York. Finally, I conclude by looking at the way in which nostalgia for *Seinfeld* has become a marker for the nostalgia inspired by the pre-Bush, pre-9/11 era, in which New York, for all the complexities explored by the show, seems now like a simpler and funnier place.

# 2 About Nothing

*Seinfeld* was famously a show 'about nothing'. The little phrase was not so much a description as an imperative: 'be about nothing!'. So being nothing was something to which the show aspired but did not always claim to have achieved. It was a way to measure that most undefinable of qualities, the funniness of a particular scene, moment or episode. The more it was about nothing the better. At the same time, nothing had two distinct senses. In the first, one might say literal sense, *Seinfeld* aspired to be a television show with no subject beyond the minutiae of everyday life. There would be no long-lost twins, no palpably oversized apartments for the characters, no narrative 'arc' to please the executives. By the time this strategy was announced to viewers in the fourth series, it had already become unsustainable. Once *Seinfeld* had become a successful show, it relied on a highly complex narrative within each episode, weaving a variety of different stories that it tried to bring to a single conclusion. Behind this literal strategy another version of being about nothing was in operation, which *Seinfeld* pursued throughout the series. In this sense, *Seinfeld* wanted to be a television comedy and nothing more, avoiding the little moral homilies and romantic entanglements so beloved of network programmers. This renunciation reveals a hidden seriousness to the show, because it did not believe that the truly important subjects, usually meaning the Holocaust, could not be treated at anything other than epic length – ideally that of the nine-hour documentary *Shoah* (1985), but at a pinch the three-and-a-half hours of the film *Schindler's List* (1993) that was often a point of

'Go along, go along'

reference for *Seinfeld*. Typically, when urged by George to 'go along' with deceiving some eavesdroppers, Jerry retorts: 'In Berlin in 1939 you'd be right there goosestepping – go along, Jerry, go along' (episode 57, 'The Outing', 1993). At the same time, its concern for everyday life was born of comedy and anxiety at once: what's the right thing to do in a given social situation and who decides? What are the rules? And if you are a Jewish immigrant, do they apply to you?

The paradox of the famous description of *Seinfeld* as a show about nothing is that it was not until the goal had been abandoned that the description was coined and stuck. In the literal sense, being about nothing meant that there should be no plot in the traditional dramatic sense, whether comic, romantic or tragic. Consequently, the show set out to be an unadorned representation of everyday life, marked by a sense of the absurd. Its function was to reveal how Jerry's stand-up comedy, shown at the beginning, middle and end of the programme, was generated by an absurd take on the experience of everyday life. The characters, sets and action of the series were intended as recognisable aspects of New York life, from interminable discussions about the best subway route to use, to the pursuit of the perfect bagel, and endless worries about real estate. Two episodes in particular came to epitomise the idea of nothingness. In the second series episode 'The Chinese Restaurant' (episode 16, 1991), Jerry, Elaine and George wait for a table in a typical Chinese restaurant before going to see the science-fiction B-movie *Plan 9 from Outer Space* (1959). George tries and fails to tell his girlfriend where they are by phone and eventually the group give up waiting, only for the table to finally be ready. In terms of truth to everyday life and absence of narrative, this episode is probably the closest to the ideal of being 'about nothing'. In using the single set of the restaurant, it feels more like theatre than television, even obeying the Greek philosopher Aristotle's rule that plays should have a unity of space, time and action. The episode uses none of the later staple locations of the show, like Jerry's apartment or Monk's coffee shop, and could still be enjoyed by someone who had no knowledge at all of the series.

21

The Chinese Restaurant

The Parking Garage

Almost its equal in minimalism was 'The Parking Garage' (episode 23, 1991), a third series episode in which all four characters search for their parked car in the vast garage attached to a shopping mall. Again, the entire episode takes place in the garage with no exterior locations. However, both Jerry and George get arrested for relieving themselves in dark corners of the garage, which creates a second dramatic space, the policeman's office. While it is scarcely beyond the ingenuity of modern theatre to create several spaces, this expansion broke Aristotle's rule concerning the unity of dramatic space that 'The Chinese Restaurant' had carefully obeyed. Although Elaine is saddled with a repetitive series of lines about a goldfish she has won that gradually dies in its plastic bag, 'The Parking Garage' is funnier than 'The Chinese Restaurant', as it pushes the experience of the everyday to absurd limits. While Jerry creates ever wilder excuses for his lack of self-control, Kramer's antics with the heavy air-conditioner he has bought exemplify the counterpoint of physical comedy that his character

Jerry caught peeing in the garage

brought to the mostly verbal comedy of the others. Kramer and George have an exchange about the fear of death in which Kramer says that there is no point in being afraid but that you should live for the moment. 'Right,' says George, 'and here I am in a shopping mall parking garage.' It's as if the show begins to sense here what a television series about nothing – as opposed to stand-up comedy or theatre – might actually be able to do. Television can create as many locations as the audience can follow (and the budget withstand), mix up time and space and still rely on that audience to follow, because we are so accustomed to the sense of 'flow' created by TV. In fact, the presumed humour works only because audiences are so accustomed to the elaborate charades of mainstream comedies that gave *Seinfeld* something to react against.

In its heyday, from the third to the seventh series (1991–6), *Seinfeld* was relaxed about itself as being television. Take the opening to one of the best-known episodes, 'The Contest' (episode 51, 1992), which won an Emmy for best episode in a comedy series. It begins with a

stand-up from Jerry about the question as to whether or not one's
parents have had sex. He holds out the thought that being adopted
would have the advantage that you would be able to deny the
possibility. In the first incarnation of *Seinfeld*, that opening might have
led to a show about one of the characters discovering their parents
having sex, a fate that awaits George later in the series. In fact, as any
fan knows, it is about the voluntary curtailment of what are elsewhere
described as 'autoerotic activities'. After an establishing shot of the
coffee-shop exterior, the episode opens with Jerry, Elaine and Kramer
eating lunch in a booth. The table is busy with glasses, plates and cutlery
and the three are 'found' engaged in lively conversation. Jerry asks
Elaine whether she thinks a person held hostage by a terrorist
organisation gets to do laundry and, just as Kramer is launching into a
riff on compulsory derobing by terrorists, a depressed George arrives.
With the table full and George's narrative about being 'caught' by his

24

Jerry and Elaine in the coffee shop

mother taking the centre of the action, the camera has to make an effort to see what's going on. In several shots, it looks over Jerry's shoulder, which intrudes into the corner of the screen. This 'over-the-shoulder' view was in fact standard for the Jerry–George coffee-shop discussion that is *Seinfeld* at its best. Most television series would try and arrange the characters so that they can be seen clearly, as in *Friends*, where the characters sat in an extended line across the coffee shop Central Perk but never in a circle. However, Jerry actively objects to this mode of seating, so that when the characters are forced to the counter, or when he finds himself sitting side by side with one person, he immediately tries to move. Displaced from its standard place opposite the actors, the camera looks as if from the adjoining tables on either side of the foursome. There is no sense of alienation created here. Rather it's fun to be part of this crowded social world and we know it's television, so we do not feel excluded by the viewpoint. In 'The Contest', as the four pledge to the honour system as a form of rules, the camera rises above the table to look down on their intertwined fingers, a viewpoint that declares the show to be television and taking advantage of it.

However, in its first two series, which ran for only thirteen episodes, *Seinfeld* struggled to escape from its literary aspirations to be more than 'just TV'. The very goal of being about nothing perhaps inadvertently[4] echoed the aspiration of the nineteenth-century French novelist Gustave Flaubert to write a book, that he described in a letter to his lover Louise Colet as

> a book about nothing, a book dependent on nothing external, which would be held together by the external strength of its style, just as the earth, suspended in the void, depends on nothing external for its support; a book which would have no subject, or at least in which the subject would be almost invisible, if such a thing is possible.

The result was his now-classic 1857 novel *Madame Bovary* that was a scandal in its day for the matter-of-fact way in which it told the story of a provincial French woman trying to raise her station in life and being

25

led into a disastrous affair. For all Flaubert's efforts to render his style the only subject of his novel, his very ability to depict accurately the social mores of its time made it at once appear to be a powerful critique of those habits. In the same way, although *Seinfeld* tried to be nothing more than comedy, it has become an icon of its time and circumstance. Ironically, it was part of the show's strategy to avoid the kind of active social commentary that had dominated Norman Lear's series *All in the Family* (1971–9) and its spin-offs *Archie Bunker's Place* (1979–83) and *Maude* (1972–8). By 1997, the *New York Times* columnist Maureen Dowd acerbically noted that *Seinfeld* had become 'our *Dorian Gray* portrait', referring to the short story by Oscar Wilde in which the portrait of Dorian Gray changes to reflect every awful action the character performs.[5]

In its first three series, *Seinfeld* owed a good deal to serious playwrights like Harold Pinter, whose style centred on everyday situations rendered comic by absurdist conversation. Perhaps unsurprisingly, *Seinfeld* became a mainstream success only when it abandoned such derivative strategies. Influenced by modernist authors like Samuel Beckett, Pinter is a British-Jewish playwright who first came to prominence with his play *The Birthday Party* (1958), in which chaos ensues after the arrival of two gangsters, one Irish and one Jewish, in a British boarding house. Their motives are never entirely clear but the play takes the situation as it is and explores its comic and dramatic possibilities to the full. In the conformist, conservative Britain of the 1950s, the appearance of such a Jewish, modernist voice was as scandalous as Flaubert had been a century earlier. *Seinfeld*'s debt to Pinter was openly acknowledged in a later episode that took the name and the reversed time-line of his 1978 play *Betrayal* and even named a character Pinter to prompt viewers to get the joke (episode 164, 'The Betrayal', 1997). However much the writers wanted to claim such connections, their own work had by that time taken a very different path. In Pinter's plays, conversation and speech often fail to communicate. The cliché of the 'Pinter-esque pause' refers to the stage direction put in by the author that there

26

should be a pause in dialogue, where the characters do nothing. The pause created gaps between the words spoken by the actors in which much of the meaning – or lack of meaning – was created. In a sitcom lasting only twenty-two minutes, the repeated pause was not an available strategy. In fact, in the early series, the actors in *Seinfeld* often spoke a very rapid dialogue, alternating back and forth between characters in a manner that is patently stagey. That is to say, rather than ask the audience to suspend its disbelief in what they were watching and imagine themselves to be a silent witness to action going on around them, the theatricality of the early episodes made the artificial nature of the experience obvious. Sometimes the characters would speak their inner thoughts in the tradition of the theatrical soliloquy from Shakespeare on, but did so in company, in the style of the modern theatre. So their thoughts are revealed to the audience but the other actors ignore them, as if they have not spoken. As the three main actors, other than *Seinfeld* himself, had extensive acting

George confronts Elaine about his showering habits

experience, this approach seems to have come naturally to them, even as it left the nominal star somewhat isolated.

The strategy began to work only when the format was, as they say, adapted for television. At this point, the characters began to minutely analyse and dissect both their own motives and those of others in fast-paced but not shotgun dialogue that discussed in everyday places and language those things that are best left unsaid in real life, such as when and why to pee in the shower, under what circumstances one may eat food out of the garbage and how to fake an orgasm. In a classic episode (episode 86, 'The Opposite', 1994), George's life begins to work when he does 'the opposite', meaning the opposite of everything he has ever done – a strategy he had in fact proposed in *The Seinfeld Chronicles*, the 1990 pilot for the series. Instead of doing what seems to come naturally to him, he consciously does the exact opposite. It begins with him reversing his usual order of a tuna sandwich on rye with a cup of coffee for lunch into chicken salad on toast with a cup of tea. This attracts the attention of a woman at the counter, who has made exactly the same order. When Elaine points out to George that he is being

George does the opposite – and it works

George refusing to go upstairs – the opposite

29

looked at, he initially scoffs at the idea that he might follow up on the
exchange of glances. Then Jerry points out that doing the opposite
would mean going to speak to her. George does so, and begins a
relationship with her that leads to his dream job with the baseball team
the New York Yankees and the end of his period of living at home with
his parents. Just as George – the fictional counterpart of producer Larry
David – turns his life around by doing the opposite, so did *Seinfeld*
become a classic series by doing the opposite. Rather than leave
mysterious pauses between everyday dialogue into which an audience
might read questions of desire, motive and personal crisis, *Seinfeld* filled
in the pause with extensive verbal analysis.

It was in the fourth series of *Seinfeld* (1992–3) that this
strategy began to work; now marketed as the 'breakthrough' series, it
represented the moment at which the show achieved a very high level
of recognition, culminating in the Emmy for Best Comedy Series.
However, there were those fans and critics who felt that the series had

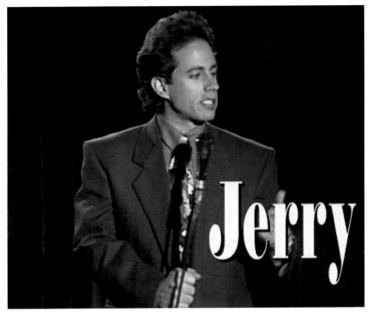

The fake title for *Jerry*

abandoned its own radical potential with a new, more viewer-friendly approach. For *Seinfeld* had now set aside its absurdist strategy for a conventional series 'arc', which is to say, a narrative running across all the episodes of a season. The success of this series followed from the public designation of the show as being 'about nothing' (episode 43, 'The Pitch', 1992). In fact, the show about nothing was *Jerry*, the show-within-the-show that was proposed to NBC and abandoned by them after its pilot, whose rise and fall constituted the narrative 'arc' of the season. This mirroring represents *Seinfeld* coming to terms with its own status as a television series, rather than being a drama like Arthur Miller's classic *Death of a Salesman* (1949), such a consistent point of reference that Jerry takes to calling George 'Biff' like Miller's character Biff Loman. The new narrative of the fourth series offered a simple link between the imagined world of stand-up and that of television when two

NBC executives approach Jerry in a comedy club and ask him to propose a series for their network. He agrees at once but has no idea what the series should be about and even entertains proposals from Kramer about a series based on a circus. George and Jerry are talking in the coffee shop that is their favoured spot for 'kibbitzing' (a Yiddish phrase that has become New York-ese for acerbic but pointless conversation) about the way salsa had replaced ketchup as the most popular condiment in America. This fact was much cited in contemporary discussions of multiculturalism but Jerry insists that it's just because people liking saying the word 'salsa'. George has an epiphany that the show for NBC should be just like what they are doing: that is to say, about nothing but everyday life. Whatever might happen to the 'real' Jerry could happen on the show-within-the-show. At a time when academia was rife with argument about post-modernism, characterised as a condition of self-referentiality in which the status of something called reality was newly open to question, *Seinfeld* was able

'People like to say "salsa"!'

'It's about nothing!'

to create just such a parodic and mirrored world precisely because it was
a sitcom, about which nobody cared because – it was about nothing.
When George signs himself up to be a writer for the pilot and Jerry
points out he has no experience, George retorts: 'Who said anything
about being a writer? It's a sitcom.' The very lack of respect afforded to
its format allowed *Seinfeld* to experiment in a way that did not alienate
its mass audience but in fact made it more popular.

When Jerry and George pitch the idea for a show about
nothing to NBC, they even suggest that one activity for the characters
might be reading. The idea of a silent, actionless activity strikes the
channel head as ridiculous and he asks why anyone would watch this?
'Because it's on TV,' replies George. His comment reveals a surface
contempt for *Seinfeld*'s own medium as a TV sitcom that prevented the
show from becoming too arrogant about its own importance. At the
same time, it shows that a programme that began as a means of
explaining the creative process of the stand-up comedian to the world

'One word – nothing!'

had come to think of itself as television. That is to say, from the viewer's point of view, television became the main point of reference rather than cinema, theatre or live performance. In the season finale of the third series, Elaine is discovered writing a screenplay for the sitcom *Murphy Brown* (1988–98), a show that became a political issue when then Vice-President Dan Quayle criticised the lead character, played by Candice Bergen, when she became a single mother. The episode concludes with Kramer, who has briefly become an actor, featuring in a cameo as Murphy Brown's secretary in which Murphy is visibly pregnant (episode 40, 'The Keys', 1992). Much later in the series, Jerry has to take a lie-detector test when his policewoman girlfriend suspects that, despite his denials, he does in fact watch the schlocky primetime soap *Melrose Place* (1992–9). The machine's accuracy forces him to confess but allows him to come out as a *Melrose Place* fan to Elaine, and the *Seinfeld* show ends with the group happily bobbing along to the show's theme tune (episode 102, 'The Beard', 1995). So the show 'about nothing' gradually morphed from being a depiction of everyday life in which people would read on TV into one where they watched TV on TV.

As such it was perhaps a better representation of American everyday life, as it set aside modernist theatricality for postmodern self-referentiality – so, instead of appreciating the technique of the monologue or the pause, you now had to know what *Melrose Place* is/was to get the joke. I should add that this sense of *Seinfeld* as becoming television is not one proposed by the writers, who attributed the new feel of the show, in the language of the industry, to a process whereby the characters themselves came to impose changes in the writing through a collective sense of their identity. At the risk of seeming absurd, I think these views can be reconciled if you are willing to accept the idea that what the characters wanted was to be TV characters and not theatrical ones. By virtue of its very ordinariness, television was better suited than theatre or cinema to represent everyday life. As Jerry says in introducing the 100th episode direct to camera (episode 100, 'Highlights of a Hundred', 1995), 'we're TV people for thirty minutes a week'. Being about nothing had become being about television.

In this and many other regards, *Seinfeld* seems to belong to an era that, however fast-paced it seemed at the time, now seems positively old-fashioned. TV-land was a known and limited terrain in the early 1990s. If a programme was on network television, it could assume a significant audience just because of that broadcast. So *Seinfeld* was allowed four series to gain an audience in a way that would be inconceivable today. By the mid-1990s, the network share of the US viewing audience dipped below 50 per cent for the first time, beginning in summer when they show mostly repeats, and later extending to the whole year. With as many as two hundred channels to choose from, and with the most inventive programming on cable channels like HBO, viewers were no longer forced to watch whatever the major networks offered them. To try and save its market share, NBC paid remarkable salaries first to Jerry Seinfeld and finally to all of the lead characters. While this seemed a little bizarre at the time, the network has not recovered from the loss of its 1990s' comedy hits like *Seinfeld*, *Frasier* and *Friends*, and has gone from being the unchallengeable number one network to third or even fourth place.

At the time, the shift in emphasis within the overall series was not without controversy. Jason Alexander went public with his doubts about the new direction, although his complaints were more about the continuing storyline of the NBC pilot than the show-within-the-show format. He felt that *Seinfeld* was character-driven rather than relying on stories and the shift would cause the programme to lose its appeal. One way of understanding this complaint would be to see it as reluctance to abandon the theatrical tradition of character acting for the televisual style of emphasising narrative. As Alexander admitted at the time, he had been wrong before and he was in fact wrong then as far as the question of popularity goes. But his point recalls a then-widespread debate about subversion and popular culture: namely, was radical change more likely if the audience were aware they were being asked to change or not? For to achieve a popular form of postmodernism on television, the most mainstream of all media, in the most mainstream of television formats, was itself an achievement. The nature of that achievement is, of course, precisely the question at stake here. At one level, for most young people of the period it seemed of vital importance to change the content of a particular medium, whether radio, theatre or television, as a means of reflecting their presence in the world. With the development first of 'niche'- and later 'narrow'-casting (content aimed at highly specific audiences) and later the Internet, with its plethora of self-publishing possibilities, such issues may now seem remote. That's in part why *Seinfeld* is a classic: it was vital in its time but that time is now past.

If it seems self-evident to think of television as television, it is in fact a surprisingly rare approach to the medium that has often been described as 'radio with pictures'. Much of television's content is, to borrow a term from the media theorist Marshall McLuhan, remediated, which is to say that it originated in a different medium and was transferred to television. So the classic BBC TV series like *Play for*

*Today* (1964–84) – a format that has now all but disappeared – was a remediation of theatre, just as the situation comedy was at first a remediation of variety theatre. *Seinfeld* was a classic example of remediation, in that it transferred the process of creating and performing stand-up comedy to television. At this point, the series began to reflect on itself as television, asking questions about what was necessary to make the lives of the characters into a television comedy. As they work on the script for their pilot, Jerry and George feel that it is too 'busy' to accommodate an Elaine character, a view that Elaine soon forced them to drop. Kramer pushes this issue to the limit when he insists on playing himself in *Jerry*. Although Jerry and George adamantly refuse, Kramer nonetheless appears to audition to play himself under his alias Martin van Nostrand, only to be thwarted by his inability to find the 'facilities' at NBC and miss his chance. This tension in the show also reflected a real question as to the future of the series that had not fully established itself after three seasons. When George

Elaine disciplines George

'Not yet!'

insists that people will watch *Jerry* just because it's on TV, the executive
Russell Dalrymple (Bob Babanal) replies, 'Not yet'. In other words,
what's on TV may be watched just because it's there but getting there
is a highly controlled and monitored process. This generates the
'normality' of ordinary television that is experienced by viewers as
boredom, as they are given no option but to watch endlessly similar
shows about hospitals, lawyers and gangs of wacky friends. Of course,
they could switch it off, but television is not going to suggest that
option.

       Once the show had become accustomed to being television,
rather than drama, it started to find itself boring and wanted to become
cinema. Throughout the later series of *Seinfeld*, there are repeated
parodies of film sequences, particularly in the little thirty-second 'teaser'
sequence that followed the last advert break. While most shows would
use this time for one last set-up and punchline, *Seinfeld* often used it to
remediate the episode into a parody of a film. For example, the end of

'The Mom and Pop Store' (episode 94, 1994) parodies a sequence from the 1969 film *Midnight Cowboy* that at once pays homage to a New York classic, makes a joke by creating an unexpected visual analogy and finally ties up a plotline about George buying a used car because he thought it had previously belonged to Jon Voight, the actor, who starred in *Midnight Cowboy* – it had in fact been owned by John Voight, the dentist. The characters are certainly aware of this last theme but the parody of the film is necessarily unacknowledged by them. The cinematic sequences express an interestingly complex sequence of desires. They put the television characters in the position of many ordinary people as aspirant movie stars, or people who would like their lives to be more like cinema and consequently less boring. Yet that aspiration is really being expressed by the writers and producers of *Seinfeld* itself. The humour of the sequences comes precisely from the absurdity of one of the 'lowest' forms of moving-image entertainment, the sitcom, claiming an affinity with the gilded world of cinema. Here any pretence at being theatre is finally abandoned. The audience not only must not suspend its disbelief in order to 'get' these sequences, they must be actively aware that they are watching television, which has no right to be playing at cinema.

Despite these complexities, *Seinfeld* was always 'about nothing' in the key sense suggested by producer Larry David that in twenty-two minutes – the actual running time of each episode – there should be 'no learning and no hugging'. Here David was distinguishing *Seinfeld* from the standard sitcom in which characters have learning experiences that they then share with a group hug at the end. If *Frasier* was the American series most prone to generating a learning experience, *Friends* could hardly get through a segment without a hug from somebody. To take a literary parallel, American print media are awash with short essays or stories, usually by graduates of MFA writing programmes, that retell a keenly observed incident from everyday life over a few hundred words and then tie it together with a moral right at the end. This writing is like airline food – it has all the appearance of a meal, but no substance and no taste. Rather than follow this standard format, David set out to create a comedy that was 'just' a comedy. To be precise, *Seinfeld* was more a comedy of manners than a romantic comedy. Most American sitcom is romantic comedy in which deferred or displaced sexual desire between leading characters is the key narrative device. For example, *Cheers* ran for over a decade (1982–93) on the premise of barman Sam Malone's (Ted Danson) endless desire for Diane, a wannabe-writer-cum-waitress (Shelley Long); and then for Rebecca (Kirstie Alley), the corporate manager of the bar once Sam's small business efforts had failed. *Friends* later kept its audience waiting to get Ross and Rachel permanently together for another decade – and then ended. By contrast, when George says to Elaine that he has always wanted to see her and Jerry get back together, she replies: 'That's because you're an idiot' (episode 159, 'The Serenity Now', 1997). The idiocy was one of comic style as well as character: if two characters in romantic comedy are desirous of each other, then that becomes the central plot motif, whether the writers originally intended it to be or not.

By refusing to be romantic, *Seinfeld* enabled itself to become a comedy of manners. Its signature move was to subject everyday life activities to a minute and logical scrutiny that demanded to know why things are the way they are and not otherwise. To take a routine that became one of Jerry Seinfeld's hallmarks as a stand-up comedian, why did airlines serve their passengers peanuts rather than something else and then why place them in tiny packages that can only be opened by the expenditure of great force, resulting in a shower of peanuts on all those in the area? Airlines have now put passengers out of their misery on most American flights by not serving anything to eat at all and offering only a tiny amount of liquid to drink in a cup filled with ice. The motive here, as before with the peanuts, is profit: peanuts were cheap, no food at all is even cheaper. Frozen water is cheaper than a drink, so lots of ice for everyone. This minute observation of distinction and difference became a hallmark of 1990s' comedy in general. Jerry Seinfeld has detected an affinity with his work in the cult film *Pulp Fiction* (1992), directed by Quentin Tarantino. One of the most discussed scenes in the film was a conversation between two hit men, played by John Travolta and Samuel L. Jackson, on their way to a job. The two killers analysed with precision the different kind of hamburgers served by McDonald's in Europe, above all the famous Royale with cheese, the French equivalent to the Quarter Pounder with cheese. The conversation ends with a whimper when Jackson tries to move on to a discussion of the European Burger King, only for Travolta to say that he didn't go to Burger King. In an increasingly homogenised world, such minor differences become the means of telling one locale from another. I recall visiting Dallas, Texas, for a conference at around this time, only for the airport van to turn on the way into a shopping mall identical in every respect to one near my house in New York. Only the weather was different, leading to the American fascination with weather reports.

There is nonetheless a profound seriousness implied in the view that twenty-two minutes is too short for moral lessons, borne out by *Seinfeld*'s perhaps Jewish or Freudian belief that social rules are the substance of civilisation.[6] An early show was entirely devoted to the question of whether or not it was permissible to manoeuvre forwards into a parking space (episode 22, 'The Parking Space', 1992). George claims that only parallel parking, involving a reverse, is acceptable, whereas his rival for the space suggests that any way in will do. A crowd gathers to discuss the issue, some siding with each of the participants but all uttering dire warnings of social collapse if their way is not followed. Newman declares to Kramer: 'You wanna know why you can't go in front first? I'll tell you why. Because it signals a breakdown in the social order. Chaos. It reduces us to jungle law.' The episode ends without a resolution of the dispute, refusing the temptation for a final comic wrap of the issue. As the series developed, it was less common for an entire show to be devoted to one rule of this kind but there were constant references to such disputes. Moments such as these fall into two types. The first poses the fundamental question as to whether a type of behaviour is disgusting or acceptable. Is it revolting or normal to dip the same chip twice? The other asks what the rules are within the category of the social: is a gift for ever or may one re-gift or even de-gift? How many dates constitute a relationship? Is a man carrying a bag effeminate

The Parking Space

'Chaos!' says Newman

or simply European? In one such typical moment, Kramer is expounding on why he insisted on claiming a penalty stroke in a golf round when his partner illegally cleaned the ball short of the putting green. When Elaine cannot see why this is important, Kramer exclaims that 'Without rules, there's chaos' (episode 88, 'The Big Salad', 1994).

However, the rules are Kramer's undoing when he runs for President of Del Boca Vista Phase III at the behest of Jerry's father. His runaway campaign is undone by his failure to wear shoes in the clubhouse. As Jerry reminds him, 'Kramer, these people work and wait their whole lives to move down here, sit in the heat, pretend it's not hot, and enforce these rules' (episode 117, 'The Wizard', 1998). Florida is the opposite to New York: in New York, you are subject to the rules but in the small world of the Florida retirement home, you can enforce them yourself and thereby stave off impending chaos. Again and again, *Seinfeld* claims the question of 'civilisation' as key to its enterprise. When George tells Jerry that he has begun eating food while having sex, Jerry replies, 'George, we're trying to have a civilisation here' (episode 160, 'The Blood', 1997). This civilisation is far from universal. When Jerry receives some free hockey tickets from a friend, he refuses to call and thank him, insisting that his repeated thanks at the moment of giving were sufficient. Kramer flies into a rage, asserting that such manners are the foundation of society, and if Jerry no longer wants to be part of society, he can 'move to the East side', meaning the wealthy, WASP-y Upper East Side of Manhattan (episode 109, 'The Face Painter', 1995). In a reversal of dominant assumptions, the domain of the civilised is restricted to the Jewish (and, in this view, therefore intellectual and politically radical) districts of the city. If that is civilisation, then it is indeed under threat as Manhattan becomes more diverse and less Jewish; in general less 'New York' in the cinematic sense of a specific location, and more 'American' in the television sense of a generically acceptable anonymous place.

These rules of everyday modern life are not defined by some eternal 'culture', which creates the codes for its members that are passed down from generation to generation. Although anthropologists once liked to attribute such patterns to so-called 'traditional' cultures such as that of the Australian Aborigines, more recently it has become clear just how much of both culture and nature are constantly in flux. To take just one example, contemporary Australians have learned to their cost that the Aboriginal peoples used to control the bush by setting fires, thereby producing the apparently 'natural' parkland look of coastal Australia. Without such controlled burns, cities like Sydney and Melbourne find themselves periodically threatened by raging bushfires. As Flaubert realised long ago, modern life is very particular and distinct in its modes of social conduct that cannot escape economic realities but operate in complex relationship to them. *Seinfeld*'s dialogues explored the boundaries that we use to create a sense of texture and meaning in everyday life. How close can you stand to someone in conversation? How loudly should you speak? Is a handkerchief an acceptable technology for treating colds? Is soup a meal and, if so, are crackers an essential part of it? Central to any such division is the boundary between the civilised and the barbaric, and at a less dramatic level, good and bad behaviour. Such concerns are particularly acute for immigrants, who may find that rules that held good at home are very different in the new country. I discovered to my cost, for instance, that whereas an invitation to coffee was not understood as a date in London circa 1989, in the detoxed recovery world of Los Angeles at the same time, any form of stimulant was equivalent to a proposition. Despite certain right-wing diatribes to the contrary, what was learned on *Seinfeld* was not how to behave but what questions to ask. The answers on the show were prompted by the funniest possible answers to various social conundrums, not as a guide to action.

43

More specifically still, anxiety about social rules is a very Jewish concern. The grand distinction between the civilised and its other was theorised by the psychoanalyst Sigmund Freud in his now-classic work *Civilisation and Its Discontents*, published in 1927. As a man in late middle age watching the swing to extremism in European politics that had already brought Mussolini's Fascists to power in Italy and would see Hitler's National Socialists triumph in 1933, Freud felt that an old and vital balance was being overturned. In his view, the establishment of civilisation relied on the renunciation of instinct. These codes are passed on to children as part of their induction to human society, as in the gradual toilet-training that teaches children to control their excretions and to keep themselves clean. In his widely used guide to child-rearing, Dr Benjamin Spock insisted on toilet-training as the foundation of modern civilisation: 'It's actually the foundation for a lifelong preference for unsticky hands, for clean clothes, for a neat home, for an orderly way of doing business.'[7] In short, toilet-training prepared the ground for what Freud would have called civilisation and even for successful capitalism. As baby-boomers raised on the Spock mantra that toilet-training is good, the *Seinfeld* generation can only look on appalled as present-day parents allow their children to continue in diapers until the age of three or older. Spock's description is also a good summary of the character of Jerry Seinfeld as presented on the show. Here is a person so neat that Kramer suspects him of being a Nazi and young women in the show assume he must be gay. He does not allow his guests to use his bathroom for a Number Two, and is so revolted by the idea that something in his house has been in the toilet that he throws away almost all his possessions before discovering that the item in question is the toilet brush (episode 150, 'The Pothole', 1997).

At one level, then, *Seinfeld* observes the world from the point of view of the wise elder, who knows that today is not as good as yesterday. A true New Yorker will always complain that New York is not what it was, no matter how old they might happen to be. At the same time, *Seinfeld* is afraid that it might be the cause of the decline and fall of the New York empire. In his essay on civilisation, Freud rather oddly attributes male superiority in many societies to a presumed earlier practice whereby men put out fires by urinating on them. In this context, I can't resist making a few observations. Why would you put out a fire in such a potentially dangerous way, rather than throwing water or earth on it? If, for some reason, urination is your preferred method, surely women, with less dangling, flammable material in that area, would be the most effective operators? Then again, why would *Homo sapiens* spend untold generations learning how to develop and cultivate fire only for some man to come and pee on it and put it out? Similar questions are put to George after he feels the need to pee in the shower at the gym and is spotted by a man in whom Elaine is interested. For George, all that matters is that he needed to go and, in contradiction to Freud and Spock alike, he maintains that holding it in is bad for you. In support, he claims to have read medical journals on the subject, prompting Jerry to ask if the said journals have 'anything to say about standing in a pool of someone else's urine?' (episode 84, 'The Wife', 1994). The comedic effect is enhanced because what is at stake is not membership of a civilisation but of a gym, because George's appropriation of the shower is a 'violation of club rules', to quote the witness.

   Such rules as these were the subject of another analysis of the rise of urban civilisation by a German Jew in the period of Nazism that has subsequently become widely influential. Written in the 1930s but only translated into English some forty years later, Norbert Elias's *The Civilizing Process* paid immense attention to exactly the kind of microscopic social practice that is the stuff of *Seinfeld*.[8] Elias understood civilisation to be a form of social practice that could be both inculcated in others and set aside. Its primary purpose, he argued, was to restrain violence so that people could live in close proximity without hurting one another. As Nazism took hold in Germany, it was clear to Elias that the civilising process was not irreversible. Elias had understood the renunciation of violence to be a symbolic process that led to wider social consequences. He concentrated in one part of his work on the evolution of the fork as an eating implement, replacing the hands and taking over from the cutting done by a knife as the means of actually eating food. For Elias, forks are a means by which the instinct to eat with the hands can be diverted into an apparently more hygienic process, and a vehicle to create a distinction between the necessary violence of cutting and the social moment of eating. You can still see people in America cut their food up first and then transfer the fork to the right hand in order to eat: Elias would have approved of this formal statement of civilised eating.

In *Seinfeld*, this discussion of the use of implements is rendered ridiculous by being centred on the eating of candy bars. At one point, Elaine observes Mr Pitt (Ian Abercrombie), her wealthy employer, eating a candy bar with a knife and fork on a plate (episode 89, 'The Pledge Drive', 1994). Hoping to make an impression in his job at the New York Yankees baseball team, George does the same and the practice soon becomes 'viral', to borrow a phrase from digital culture. That is to say, as the programme continues, we see all manner of people whom the characters do not know personally eating candy bars with a knife and fork. To add to the silliness, the knives and forks are metal and the plates china, a very unlikely place setting for cookies and candy bars. Uncertain of what they have done, the characters start to feel like outsiders in their own society, as older people often do, prompting Elaine to jump to her feet in a crowded café and shout 'What's the matter with you people? Have you all gone mad?' in seeming reference to the classic 1956 horror movie *Invasion of the Body Snatchers*. *Seinfeld* brought this very Jewish sensibility of being uncertain how to proceed in social situations that are not domestic to a national (Gentile) audience. It struck a chord because the emergent model of globalisation in the 1990s was creating a widespread sense of a fake or virtual reality that led to a new uncertainty concerning the global rules. For European philosophers like Jean Baudrillard and Umberto Eco, America had become a society in which it was impossible to tell a copy from an original. More worryingly still, there were now copies that had no original. That is to say, while we can all recognise a drawing of Mickey Mouse, there is no original Mickey Mouse from which to copy this drawing, as he was an animated character created only by the assemblage of thousands of drawings, none of which were indispensable. For Baudrillard, this meant that Disneyland was not the exception to modern American everyday life but its most perfect incarnation.

In this view, the uncertainty of post-modern everyday life was dramatised as tragedy, later epitomised in the Baudrillard-quoting movie *The Matrix* (1999). *Seinfeld* treated it as comedy with great effect. For the most part, the new social relations produced by global change were to be absorbed, discussed and endlessly negotiated, rather than negated. In this sense, *Seinfeld* represented its moment very well, as one of a generalised optimism about the possibilities of the new global regime, even if its workings were barely understood. However, even in *Seinfeld*'s world, the new globalisation can intrude with harsh consequences. Early in the series, Jerry strikes up a relationship with a local restaurant owner named Babu (Brian George), a Pakistani immigrant. As the restaurant is not doing well, Jerry suggests that Babu make it into a Pakistani restaurant, as there are no other such eateries in the neighbourhood, thinking to himself, 'How bad can it be?'. His ignorance is a little odd, because even during this period, there were plenty of Indian and Pakistani restaurants in New York, although they were concentrated in the East Village on Sixth Street. Given the dangerous reputation this area had acquired in the 1980s, it might have been off the radar of an Upper-West-sider like Seinfeld. However, the restaurant fails again, leading Jerry to get Babu a job in his local coffee shop and an apartment in his building. It all goes wrong when Jerry goes out of town and has Elaine collect his mail. Due to an error by the postman, Babu's visa renewal form is placed in Jerry's mailbox and, because Elaine did not give him the letters promptly, Babu is arrested for failing to renew his visa (episode 55, 'The Visa', 1993). Despite Jerry's best efforts – frustrated by his misrepresentation of himself as a dark, disturbed character to their immigration lawyer in order to facilitate George's chances of dating her as 'the funny guy' – Babu ends up being deported for visa irregularities. The episode ends with Babu regaling a friend with the story back in Pakistan, using his signature line 'He's a very bad man, very bad'. Looking at the episode now, it seems rather less funny to see an angry Pakistani man vowing 'vengeance' on America, as Babu does, after 9/11 and the invasion of Afghanistan. In early 2007, north-west Pakistan has been identified as the site of new Taliban and al-Qa'ida training camps, while the Bush administration pursues its folly in Iraq. In one of the first episodes of the series (episode 4, 'Male Unbonding', 1990), Jerry had riffed on the idea of being asked

47

48    'A very bad man!'

to perform by Hezbollah at their 'terrorism convention', a joke no
television comedian would risk today.

    *Seinfeld* finished its first run in 1998. Arguably, this was the
last time that the sitcom was a dominant form on American network
television. With the subsequent development of reality television and
other forms of interactive television like the remarkably popular
*American Idol*, no network comedy has achieved *Seinfeld*'s level of
success and centrality to the culture. In fact, *Seinfeld*'s dissection of the
everyday was soon subjected to a much-vaunted public attack as being
the promoter of a cynical irony that undermined the public sphere and
the possibility of change. The author of this broadside[9] was one
Jedediah Purdy, a then twenty-four year-old young fogey looking to
make a name for himself. Purdy targeted *Seinfeld* as 'irony incarnate'.
In his view, irony prevents words from meaning what they are intended
to mean, unlike in his native West Virginia, where 'our words sat

squarely on things that we knew in common'. Although he knows that modernity implies the inevitable mingling of disparate cultures that do not have things in common, Purdy hankers for the days when 'each white man believed almost instinctively that he was as good, as deserving, as full of possibility as anyone else'. Purdy's reading of *Seinfeld* makes the mistake of taking the characters' actions in the show to be its intended meaning, contrary to the show's declared motto 'no hugging, no learning'. It is even harder to take seriously his proposal that two bumper stickers reading 'Magic Happens' and 'Mean People Suck' add up to 'what might be called the anti-*Seinfeld* position'.[10] Purdy got his reading of *Seinfeld* completely the wrong way around, as Jerry Seinfeld himself pointed out on *Saturday Night Live*. *Seinfeld*'s comedy was not at all about refusing the possibility that words have a specific meaning. It spent a great deal of time trying to decide what those meanings were. Nor did it refuse 'to identify strongly with any project, relationship or aspiration'. On the contrary, *Seinfeld* took being funny very seriously. Purdy's attack sat well with the political campaigns of 2000 in which the Bush/Cheney contingent promised to 'say what we mean and mean what we say' as part of their project to 'restore honor to the White House'. After their election victory, it was widely commented that the grown-ups had come back into power, echoing *Seinfeld*'s fear that it was just child's play compared to the work of 'men'. Purdy's attack on the show was much recalled in the aftermath of the 9/11 attacks when it became commonplace to assert that irony was over. To think of the regime that brought us Abu Ghraib, Guantanamo and widespread torture as the 'adult' pursuit of 'honor' is to realise that irony cannot be so easily written out of the script of everyday life. At the same time, to reduce *Seinfeld* to an exercise in irony is to miss the subtlety of its mix of verbal and physical comedy. It's time to look more closely at the funniness of being funny.

49

# 3 Funny Guy

It is a truth universally acknowledged, as Jane Austen might have had it, that most of what is presented on television as comedy is not funny. Some sitcom is so dire, it's hard to imagine that even its writers really thought it was funny. Move beyond this 'universal' rule and agreement quickly ends. What is funny? Who decides? For most television viewers, these theoretical questions are simply decided by watching – if you keep watching, it's good enough. For professional comedians, the question of funniness is both central and unanswerable. *Seinfeld* made the question of what's funny or not a key theme of its own practice, playing off the interaction of the different styles of Jerry Seinfeld and Larry David. It is notorious that any discussion of humour is by its nature not going to be funny. A joke that has to be explained isn't funny and estimations of humorousness are even less so. No book has ever been less funny than Sigmund Freud's *Jokes and Their Relation to the Unconscious* (1905), for example. At the same time, writing in 2007, as the war in Iraq has metamorphosed into a civil war, leading the US President to make threats against Iran as a compensatory strategy, and as the planet warms up to boiling point, it's hard to see the present as a funny time. It is noticeable that the most successful new American comedy format has been the interplay of news and humour on Jon Stewart's *The Daily Show* (1996–) and its spin-off *The Colbert Report* (2005–) that parody news reporting and the media. While British humour has become newly funny in programmes like *The Office* and *Little Britain*, it seems as if the end of the twentieth century was the end of innovative network television humour in the United States. This turn away from comedy is the indicator of a newly authoritarian public culture of religiosity, prurience and censorship.

Comedy is an important indicator of the state of political and cultural life. To make the claim boldly, comedy is democratic because it relies on dialogue and exchange, whereas propaganda, like pornography, is one-dimensional.[11] That is to say, propaganda and pornography are dedicated to one end, whether political or erotic, whereas comedy involves complexity and audience response. Comedy does not have a monopoly on the democratic form, but without comedy there is no democracy. This distinction is foundational, in that it is part of the formation of Western notions of both theatre and politics. Western theatre has been divided into tragedy and comedy since the annual competitions of the ancient Greek theatre in Athens. From the early fifth century BCE onwards, the Athenian magistrates organised an annual contest of five comedies, replacing earlier local performances undertaken by volunteers in the local districts of Athens. Played by actors wearing masks, prosthetic bellies and penises, the comedies satirised politics, sexual mores and perhaps above all religion and superstition. Greek comedy went through several stages, now known as Old, Middle and New comedy. Old comedy gave a central place to a chorus of characters who mediated the action for the audience, often speaking to them directly. In the transition from Old to Middle comedy around 400 BCE, the role of the chorus was reduced, and the drama became more associated with the vicissitudes of everyday life, especially love affairs and confidence tricks. In this form, ancient comedy seems immediately recognisable and familiar, even having affinities with modern observational comedy like *Seinfeld* and political satire.

Aristotle, the ancient philosopher and theorist of theatre, famously defined the role of tragedy as provoking a 'catharsis', which is to say an expunging of the passionate emotions of pity and fear by watching an imitation of death and disaster.[12] As the modern sense of the word implies, catharsis was held to cleanse the mind and thereby improve it. However, Aristotle's theory of comedy has either been lost

51

or was never fully elaborated. In the *Poetics*, he claimed that comedy is 'an imitation of men worse than the average; worse, however, not as regards any and every sort of fault, but only as regards one particular kind, the ridiculous'.[13] In his novel *The Name of the Rose* (1983), the historian and literary theorist Umberto Eco suggested that comedy produces a catharsis of the ridiculous. Comedy is doubly important (and here Eco is writing in the pretended voice of Aristotle): 'inasmuch as – alone among the animals – man is capable of laughter'.[14] In short, we are never more human and more alike than when laughing. In Eco's story, the blind librarian Jorge keeps his unique copy of Aristotle's book on comedy hidden because, he says; 'if laughter is the delight of the plebeians, the license of the plebeians must be restrained and humiliated, and intimidated by sternness'.[15] Eco's allegory of the radical potential inherent in ancient comedy was of course also meant to refer to the then-present of the neo-conservative 1980s and has become relevant again today.

The point here is not to claim that *Seinfeld* might be classic in the sense that Aristophanes is classic: we will have to wait and see if media studies classes in 5000 CE are still discussing it for that parallel to hold good. Instead, following Eco, I'm making the more audacious suggestion that there must be comedy for there to be democracy. Comedy acted as one of the balances within the Athenian democratic system, designed to forestall the rise of tyranny. The lesson of tragedy is resignation in the face of fate, whether divine or human. In comedy, what Eco calls a catharis of the ridiculous can operate in two forms. In the tradition of carnival, the possibility of the ridiculous is sated by its extravagant experience. In comedy proper, new arenas for ridicule are generated by what Eco-as-Aristotle called 'the irrelevant and the inconsequent ... [and] from play on words'. The catharsis here is more subtle: it expunges the ridicule heaped on ordinary people by their superiors and by themselves. If tragedy suggests to the people that they should know their place, comedy reminds democratic leaders to mind theirs. Comedy draws its energy from the hope that such temporary reversals can sometimes be made permanent and subverts the

The Improv Comedy Club

53

pretensions of the powerful by making them ridiculous. Today it is often
claimed that many young people in the United States get their news from
satirical television programmes like *The Daily Show* rather than from
network news broadcasts, which have a markedly older audience. While
the mouthpieces of corporate morality pretend to see in this shift a sign
of cultural decadence, it is in fact one of the last hopes for democracy in
the American Empire.

    *Seinfeld*'s form of comedy emerged from its own particular
place and time and from a certain form of democracy. In the New York
comedy clubs of the late 1970s and early 1980s, the audience was
intimately involved in determining the success of a performer. At clubs
like Catch a Rising Star, where Jerry Seinfeld made his debut in July
1976, amateurs performed in ten-minute slots for no other reward than
audience approval. Many performers found themselves booed off, or in
the term of the time 'gonged', referring to the ritual at The Gong Club,
derived from the television programme *The Gong Show* (1976–80;

1988–9), where the MC would ring a gong when it was felt that an act should end. Should audience approval be gained over a period of time, you could move gradually up the ladder to more favourable slots and perhaps ultimately cross over to the paid performances. While these payments were not going to make anyone rich, they were enough for a single person to get by. In 1980, comedians in Los Angeles staged a comedy strike to ensure that all performers on the bill were at least paid a nominal amount. Today, as a sign of the different times, aspirant comedians have to earn a place on the roster by persuading passers-by to pay for admission to the comedy club where they wish to perform, meaning that they in effect pay the club for the chance to work. What was really at stake then and now for the novice comedian was the much harder task of attaining the professional approval of fellow comedians, whether performing on the same bill or just hanging out. In any performance, there were in effect two audiences – the 'lay' audience, who paid for admission, and the 'professional' comped and guest list audience, which would be joined by those performers on the bill who were waiting their turn or who had performed already. This group was usually found around the bar at the back of the room. Here performances were appreciated for nuance, improvement and daring in a way that did not necessarily accord with the views of those seeing the work for the first time.

54

   *Seinfeld* was the product of an interaction between two comics who appealed primarily to each of these two different audiences. Producer Larry David was a classic 'professional' performer, who had relatively little popular standing. He was seen as the 'conscience' of the comedy scene, standing for integrity and the pursuit of new ideas over professional advancement. He was known for such routines as berating audience members who talked during sets and even entire audiences for failing, as he saw it, to appreciate the humour of a set or a segment. Perhaps unsurprisingly, he had struggled professionally, despite working for one season on the writing team of *Saturday Night Live* and winning small parts in two Woody Allen movies, *Radio Days* (1987) and *Another Woman* (1988). Although his material was regarded as the best around, he was held to lack the stagecraft, structure and temperament to break out of the club scene. By contrast, when the television series was first mooted in 1988, Jerry Seinfeld enjoyed phenomenal popularity, which came with a professional recognition for his skills even if he was seen as lacking 'depth' or daring. A review of the period by Lawrence Christon of the *Los Angeles Times* criticised Seinfeld's act in these terms: 'He's expressive. He's clear. And he's completely empty … Seinfeld pays homage to insignificance, and he does it impeccably.' At this time, with the comedic high ground established by such performers as Andy Kaufman and Richard Pryor, who were completely identified with their material, *Seinfeld*'s ironic distance did not yet convince by itself. Combined with David's passion, anger and lack of interest in doing the right thing, it somehow worked. *Seinfeld* was the product of the New York scene, and the interaction of two writers from that scene. This simple act of doubling created a series of resonances that added up to something unexpectedly original.

'Who's better than you?'

Jerry Seinfeld once described New York as a 'gymnasium of irritation'. Whereas in Los Angeles people might undertake therapy or do yoga to erase their stress, while in London it might be ignored as part of the codes of politeness, in New York people work on their irritation. They exercise it. The root of New York irritation is a democratic principle, expressed in the question 'You think you're better than me?'. To which the implied follow-up is 'I know you do, but you're not'. George and Jerry rehearse just such a routine on their way in to see the NBC executives to pitch their idea for *Jerry* (episode 43, 'The Pitch', 1992). The phrase 'funny guy' that I took for the title of this chapter is addressed to Jerry by George in the middle of a flight to India because George knows that Jerry has slept with his girlfriend Nina. So even the ultimate comedian's compliment is used in the show as an insult (episode 164, 'The Betrayal', 1997). The parodic maximum expression of this very New York characteristic is the character known as the Soup

'No soup for you!'

Nazi. Known for punishing people for misbehaving in his shop by refusing to serve them, or depriving them of bread to go with their soup, his cry of 'No soup for you!' became an instant catchphrase (episode 116, 'The Soup Nazi', 1995).

These questions were central to a significant moment in the history of *Seinfeld*, namely the first episode of the fifth series, when it took over the coveted nine o'clock time slot from *Cheers*. In this heavily promoted episode, everything turns around truth and self-representation. Jerry's opening stand-up chastises scientists for working on developing seedless watermelon when diseases like AIDS remain uncured. He speculates that their ultimate goal is to get rid of the rind as well so that the fruit will grow directly into a cup. As so often in *Seinfeld*, the seemingly incidental question of fruit becomes the way of linking the different stories in the episode. The action opens at Monk's, where Elaine serves up the bombshell that she had faked orgasm – the word was used in the show – with Jerry not just once but every time. Kramer later consoles Jerry with the revelation that he too has faked it, 'when it's enough already and you just want to get some sleep'. At that moment, he is revolted by a mealy peach he is eating and decides to return it to the fruit stand. Joe the fruit seller is so outraged by this presumption that Kramer is better than him that he bans him from the store with the classic local line: 'I don't want your business!', implying he would rather starve than take money from someone who looks down on him. When Jerry tries to buy fruit for Kramer, his performance in the shop is so patently fake that Joe recognises Kramer's fruit preferences and bans him from the store in turn. George, who has been having trouble performing with his current girlfriend Karen (Lisa Edelstein), is sent to the store to buy fruit for two, and a piece of mango restores his vigour. However, he interprets Karen's response in the resulting encounter as a fake and she angrily rejects him. Meanwhile Jerry and Elaine have tried a rematch in order for Jerry to conjure up the elusive orgasm, only to find that he is also unable to perform. The episode closes as Elaine asks if he has any mango left and Jerry's eyes light up with anticipation. The closing stand-up tied the episode together with Jerry's well-known skit about female

57

orgasm being like a car crash: 'in the end my body was thrown clear' (episode 63, 'The Mango', 1993). Or was it faked?

The classic film of New York everyday life *Naked City* (1948) begins with the line 'There are eight million stories in the naked city', meaning each person has a story they think could and should be made into a feature film. Using a film noir style, the tales in *Naked City* were based on everyday life. In a sense, *Seinfeld* is the comedic fulfilment of that idea, as it claimed that the events of any person's day in New York could be the basis for a show. For that reason, the spirit of New York's unofficial cinematographer of the period, Woody Allen, is present throughout the show. It was the not-so-secret ambition of every New Yorker to feature in one of his films and Kramer comes close to fulfilling it. At first incorporated as an extra by virtue of his striking appearance, Kramer soon gets promoted to a speaking role with the line 'These

Kramer in his dumb phase

George in his smart phase

Normal George

pretzels are making me thirsty' (episode 28, 'The Alternate Side', 1991).
All the cast rehearse various ways of saying it, ready at any moment to
step into the film. Needless to say, Kramer soon klutzes his way out of
his part, and the dream remains unfulfilled. The way in which Jason
Alexander interpreted the part of George in the early series of *Seinfeld*
was a thinly veiled copy of Woody Allen's neurotic and nervous style, as
Alexander has acknowledged. But it was only once the show had turned
away from such imitation that it found its own comedic style.

The shift can be seen in the changing characters of George and
Kramer. In the first two series, Kramer is rather slow-witted, often
making mistakes. He frequently appears unshaven and his clothing has
no particular style. George on the other hand is Woody Allen incarnate,
smart and nervous. In one early episode, he uses the word 'anathema' to
the bafflement of Jerry and the others. Of course in the later versions, the
position is reversed. Kramer has snap and sartorial style, even becoming
a Calvin Klein underwear model, while George transforms into a loser,

Kramer Komedy

Richards performed these stunts himself

wearing clothes a size too small and obsessing about his baldness. In Michael Richards's hands, Kramer displays an alternative form of physical comedy within the show that complemented its otherwise verbal style. From his signature dramatic entrances to the variety of prat-falls and other exaggerated movements and gestures he made, Kramer was a character in the tradition of Buster Keaton and other physical comics. Like Keaton, Richards performed his own stunts, breaking a rib on at least one occasion. In the more restricted time available for a tele-vision shoot, the stunts had to be worked out in two takes rather than the ten or more often used in feature films. The skills required to create such effects had to be concealed with great care. For example, Jason Alexander had enjoyed a successful Broadway musical career that could occasionally be glimpsed when George sings or dances far better than he has any right to be able to do. The panoply of narcissism and failure that

surrounded characters like Kramer and George gave the actor Jerry
Seinfeld the space to create a character 'Jerry' whose primary function
was to comment on the actions of others. By refusing to create a perspective of identification, *Seinfeld* made irony into a form of dialogue, the
perspective of the diasporic citizen who is from both there and here.

These changes were by no means the end of the process.
Unusually for a sitcom, the *Seinfeld* viewer was not asked to identify
with the characters as such, whose fortunes and personalities changed
week by week, much as the humour did. In fact, the characters were not
even particularly likeable, especially as the series went on. The actors
have often stressed that people were not supposed to like the characters,
a point drummed home by the series finale, in which they are put on trial
for violation of a Good Samaritan law (episodes 179–80, 'The Finale,
parts 1 and 2', 1998). This fictional law required people to assist anyone
in distress, which the group violated by watching a man getting mugged,
not helping but videotaping the robbery and making sarcastic comments
throughout. During the trial, a parade of former guest characters empha-
sises the point that the main characters were really not supposed to be
thought of as role models. By contrast, hits like *M\*A\*S\*H* (1972–83) or
*Cheers* depended on each character being either likeable or not, articu-
lating a constant and specific point of view, epitomised in *Cheers*' case by
Norm (George Wendt) sitting in the same seat at the bar for ten years.

As a stand-up comedian, Jerry Seinfeld has expressed a passion
for what he calls 'pure' comedy that stays true to its roots. Comedy and
acting are imagined as different, with one not guaranteeing the other.
The character Jerry panicked in the run-up to the fictional pilot for the
same reason, although the actual acting shortcomings of Jerry Seinfeld
had been more apparent in earlier seasons. Neither George's therapist
nor Elaine found the pilot *Jerry* to be funny, although they would not
say why. The sequences shown to us as part of *Seinfeld* are not in fact
that funny, a typically counter-intuitive Larry David move. Whereas
most sitcoms would have made the pilot as funny as possible, *Seinfeld*
makes it less funny than the 'everyday life' that surrounds it. After the
pilot *Jerry* has been screened, the new head of NBC passes on the option

to make a series out of the show, because of her belief that 'stand-ups can't act' (episode 64, 'The Pilot, part 2', 1993). With the pilot *Jerry* dropped, the writers of *Seinfeld* escaped having to develop a consistent narrative arc for the remaining season, and it only re-emerges as a device to end the entire series. The success of the idea of a show about nothing, which had made *Seinfeld* both a critical and a ratings winner by the end of its fourth series, now enabled it to pursue its particular sense of comedy without fear of cancellation. The move away from narrative back to dialogic exchange enabled *Seinfeld* to become a pure ensemble television comedy, whose claim to be the source for one stand-up comedian was no longer taken too seriously.

*Seinfeld* consistently questioned its own funniness as a form of existential worry: Is the show still funny? Was it ever funny? For instance, Jerry finds himself dogged by another comic Kenny Bania (Steve Hytner). So awful is Bania's material that Jerry agrees to be his mentor and write new material for him. These segments are in themselves parodies of the observational style, such as a riff on Ovaltine – 'Why is it called Ovaltine? The mug is round. The jar is round. They should call it round tine.' Bania excitedly greets this material as 'gold', even as the audience laughs at the weakness of the joke. To Jerry's consternation, Bania starts to do well with this material, leading George to declare that 'Bania is the voice of a new generation – my generation'. All Jerry can do is protest that he and George were in the same year at school so they are of the same generation (episode 140, 'The Fatigues', 1996). In a later conversation with Kramer, Jerry says that he thinks another performer, Sally Weaver, played by stand-up Kathy Griffin, should give up as she does not have what it takes. When Kramer reports this advice to Sally, she is on the verge of doing so when Jerry intervenes and tells her 'We all stink' and she should persevere (episode 169, 'The Cartoon', 1998). This rebuff provides her with perfect material and she devises a set around the theme 'Jerry Seinfeld is the Devil'. This show is such a hit that she gets a cable special, which the character Jerry has failed to do. For Jerry's enemy Newman, 'it's so refreshing to see a show that's [pause] about something'.

63

One distinctive aspect of the mature *Seinfeld* style was its cross-generational humour. At a simple level, this entailed a level of reference to popular culture of a much earlier period than the 1990s. Jerry has an obsession with Superman, a character that seemed distinctly dated despite the successful Christopher Reeve movie in 1987. His favourite baseball players include 1950s' legend Joe Di Maggio and Mickey Mantle, who stopped playing in 1968. While these were certainly familiar names to Yankees fans, there is a certain oddity about a group of young-ish professionals kicking them around in the 1990s. In turn, at a professional level, the actors in *Seinfeld* made frequent reference to the early cinematic comedy team Laurel and Hardy as well as Abbott and Costello of the 1950s. Their films were staples of children's television in Britain in the 1960s, when I was growing up, and it may in part account for why *Seinfeld* seemed so immediately funny and transparent to me despite its very local New York references. It's hard to imagine decades-old black-and-white comedy on CBeebies, the BBC digital channel for children, or its American equivalent, Nickelodeon, these days. They are out there on a cable TV channel aptly named TVLand, narrow-casts watched only by people of a certain age – like me. Perhaps the old idea of broadcasting is itself a niche idea now.

*Seinfeld* was closest to *The Jack Benny Program*, screened from 1950 to 1965 and derived from the radio programme of the same name that had begun broadcasting in 1932. In both formats, Jack Benny (originally Benjamin Kubelsky) played himself as a 'straight-man' lead character playing off a wise-cracking woman he was not dating. The significant difference is that in *Seinfeld*, Jerry's male sidekick is the Jewish/Italian/nebbish George, rather than the African-American butler Rochester, who assisted Benny. There is a curious double-bind at stake here. On the one hand, as many critics pointed out at the time and since, *Seinfeld* had no regular African-American characters, but on the other, Rochester (played by Eddie Anderson) was a stereotyped servant, who often performed song-and-dance routines that bordered on minstrelsy – ironically, the character was first slated to be played by Jewish actor Benny Rubin.[16] There is a reference to this history in the storyline of the show-within-the-show proposed to NBC, in which a judge sentences a traffic offender who has no money to work as Jerry's butler. This kind of interaction was part of *Seinfeld*'s internal dynamic, a set of references to other comedy designed for the person in the know and revealed to the mass audience only with the advent of DVD commentary and captions.

    *Seinfeld* made no overt reference to the digital culture of its day, despite Jerry's sometimes Mac sometimes Windows computer, but instead revelled in the apparently outdated comedy of earlier periods. George is appalled when a clown at a party for children has not heard of Bozo the Clown, the famous performer of the 1960s. Kramer, needless to say, is afraid of clowns. There were jokes in *Seinfeld* that seemed to come from an earlier time, such as a repeated obsession with deafness, whether permanent or temporary. The deaf actress Marlee Matlin appears in one episode as a lip-reader who can interpret a conversation with George's former girlfriend to find out why she dumped him (episode 70, 'The Lip Reader', 1993). In another episode, the inaudible 'low-talking' of Kramer's girlfriend requires Jerry to wear a pirate's puffy shirt on the *Today* show, while promoting a benefit for the homeless (episode 66, 'The Puffy Shirt', 1993). Yet another episode had Elaine turn down a desired date with the dentist Tim Whatley because she was temporarily deafened by a Dixieland jazz band (episode 94, 'The Mom and Pop Store', 1994). There were jokes about ugly babies, fat people, thin people, parents, children and all the old staples of a vaudeville stand-up comedian. There's a recurring storyline about 'little people' (people of restricted growth) and their role in the entertainment industry. When Jerry is trying to think of a theme for his pilot, Kramer encourages him to do a show set in a circus, so that he can have a cast of 'freaks', because 'people want to look at freaks, Jerry'. Despite all this, *Seinfeld* was not offensive as comedy, perhaps because it made its intent to offend so obvious. At the same time, a show that disparaged its own lead characters to the extent that *Seinfeld* did could hardly be accused of claiming superiority over others.

    *Seinfeld* not only made use of references to earlier comedy, it incorporated an older generation of comedy actors who added an extra

65

The *Seinfeld* parents

dimension to the show. At first, the show featured only Jerry's parents, playing a rather standard Jewish family in which the mother cannot believe that anyone does not like her son and the father's protests are marginalised or ignored. With the addition of George's parents, Frank and Estelle Costanza, played by Jerry Stiller and Estelle Harris, a new set of possibilities emerged. Take Frank's delineation of the cup sizes in which bras are available to his despairing son. On paper the lines 'You got the A, the B, the C and the D. The D is the biggest' seem uninspiring (episode 68, 'The Sniffing Accountant', 1993). Add in a New York accent so heavy as to be almost toxic, Stiller's air of borderline hysteria even when seated, and his ecstatic body language, and the sequence becomes pure comedy. In several sequences involving Stiller the other characters are visibly laughing, unable to restrain themselves for every take. As the characters developed, the parents had their own rivalries and contests, most notably when the senior *Seinfeld*s implausibly assure the Costanzas that their vast new condominium development in Florida has no more vacancies. Stung by this transparent deceit, Frank Costanza at once declares that he will move heaven and earth to move into Del Boca Vista because 'they don't want us there' (episode 126, 'The Shower Head', 1996). In the mature *Seinfeld*, spite is one of the major motivations of the characters. It is the irritation of New York life taken to a degree of refinement, in which you may not be able to get what you want but you can prevent someone else from doing so, or at least spoil their day. When Jerry tries to return a jacket he has bought because Elaine is now dating the salesman, he asserts that the reason is simply 'spite'. The manager refuses to accept this as a valid motive and when Jerry says the reason is in fact that the jacket does not fit, he points out that 'you already said spite' (episode 129, 'The Wig Master', 1996). Once spite is out, it cannot be retracted.

There is an egalitarianism hidden in all this bluster that reaches the surface of *Seinfeld* only on certain occasions. In one episode, Jerry and Elaine are returning from St Louis to New York by plane but because of a reschedule, he gets a seat in first class and she is consigned to the travelling hell of 'coach', which 'will be about as nice as travelling by coach for several thousand miles'. Seated next to an improbably beautiful model, Jerry enjoys wine and ludicrously fine cuisine – Dover sole in white wine sauce with 'just a pinch of saffron' – while Elaine finds herself in the dreaded middle seat next to a guy who's carrying all his bags (episode 52, 'The Airport', 1992). As she squeezes out to go to the toxic toilet, Elaine decides to try and sneak past the curtain into first. Her expulsion is swift and inglorious, prompting her to declare, 'You know, society shouldn't be divided into classes!' This line is funny because it is usually impossible to say such things in the United States, where any mention of class is seen as tantamount to socialism. For instance, when Democrats argued that Bush's tax cuts were redistributing wealth from the poor to the rich, it was they who were saddled with the accusation of waging class war. In America, everyone is middle class, from the (increasingly rare) factory worker to the deliberately low-key billionaire like Bill Gates of Microsoft. Only aircraft seating makes the actual divisions of American society briefly visible, as in the different experiences of Jerry and Elaine. No US carrier would imitate the cheeky Virgin Airlines and call its expensive seats 'Upper Class'. Later Kramer imports some Dominicans to New York in an attempt to pass them off as Cuban cigar rollers. To make the effort convincing, he gives them a crash course in Communism, only to see it rebound on him when the immigrant workers find this radicalism all too attractive, culminating with their hijack of a plane (on which Elaine is again a coach-class passenger), to take them to Cuba (episode 151, 'The English Patient', 1997).

In one episode, the narrative centres around a reading of Communism. Elaine has a new boyfriend, Ned, a Communist who reads the *Daily Worker* and evokes the still controversial topic of the blacklist. When director Elia Kazan was given a lifetime achievement Oscar in 1999, despite having named names to the House UnAmerican Activities Committee in 1952 at the height of the anti-Communist frenzy inspired by Senator Joe McCarthy, many in the audience, such as actor Nick Nolte, refused to applaud. In *Seinfeld*, the blacklist morphed into a delivery list for a favoured Chinese restaurant. In this episode, Kramer is working as a department-store Santa and finds himself attracted to socialism when Ned points out to him the poor working conditions and benefits that come with this position. Kramer's Santa career comes to an end when he tells the children who ask for presents that they have been made by other children in sweatshop conditions, leading one child to jump up and cry 'Santa's a Commie!' (episode 96, 'The Race', 1994). Towards the end of the series, it is even revealed that Kramer's unusual lifestyle has been a product of his decade-long strike from the legendary New York bagel shop H&H Bagels (episode 166, 'The Strike', 1997). None of this makes *Seinfeld* an activist show, although Jerry Seinfeld did organise a benefit show after the 1991 riots caused by the Rodney King verdict, in which white police officers were acquitted of charges despite videotape evidence that they beat him.[17]

However, class-related politics has rarely been the subject of television comedy, with certain exceptions such as the 1970s' British series *Citizen Smith* (1977–80) that centred on the life of a would-be

68

revolutionary, albeit with the intent of satirising the lead character Wolfie Smith. Series like *Roseanne* (1988–97) that depicted working-class everyday life stayed away from anything that might be called class-consciousness. In contemporary America – or Britain for that matter – there is not a sufficiently substantial radical culture for such a parody to have purchase. This is not to say that there is no class in America. Rather, as Freud argued, when certain things are at once so secret and important that they cannot be overtly acknowledged by the conscious mind, they are displaced onto other things. In Freud's famous theory of dreams, the images that appear to be nonsense or ridiculous in dreaming are in fact displaced and distorted clues to such secrets. In accentuating the ridiculous side of such displacements, we produce comedy. This connection between laughter and displacement is one of the reasons why it is hard to write about comedy in a way that keeps the humour alive. Prose wants a narrative that proceeds in a straight line but comedy jumps sideways to create its sense of surprise, an element that Jerry Seinfeld has identified as central to his humour.

My sense of *Seinfeld* is that the recurring indicators of class were not just coincidence but an acknowledgment of a key element in American life. They are important because they allow us to see *Seinfeld*'s persistent preoccupations with the comedy of ethnicity as a displacement of this secret drama. American comedy displaces class into 'race' and ethnicity. The cultural analyst Stuart Hall has taken Freud's theory of displacement (in which a dream symbol represents something other than what it appears to be) to suggest that class is actually lived through 'race'. Let us note at once that what is persistently called 'race' does not exist, as repeatedly demonstrated by scientists who have shown that there are no significant biological differences between people, even between those with visible distinctions such as skin colour. Nonetheless, 'race' persists and may even be strengthening as a cultural component of American life. There have been persistent efforts to connect genetics to race, and the aftermath of Hurricane Katrina in 2005 made the politics of ethnicity and poverty all too visible. That is to say, what appear to be 'facts' of socio-economic life are displaced into 'facts' of biology so that in modern America, economic disadvantage very often coincides with membership of an ethnic minority. While that could be read as a question of class difference, it is interpreted as one of 'race', centring on such questions as why Asian-Americans do better in school than African-Americans. Although the majority of the poor are white, popular terminology such as 'white trash' indicates that racialising theory has accommodated this problem by categorising impoverished whites as failures of their own ethnicity, garbage fit only for disposal. Needless to say, such characterisations prompt intense anger that is often displaced into comedy or deflected by remarks such as 'it's only a joke'. The success or failure of many comedians depends on the ability to negotiate this relay between anger and humour successfully.

It was no coincidence that one of the most contested areas in the debate over multiculturalism in the 1990s was the question of racialised humour. For some people, it was essential to be able to make reference to people's ethnicity in order to be funny and any sense that such jokes were not allowed led to accusations of 'political correctness'. Recently, comedians like Sarah Silverman – who played one of Kramer's girlfriends on *Seinfeld* (episode 146, 'The Money', 1997) – and Sacha Baron-Cohen have turned this debate on its head by parodying the intense nervousness with which such discussions are conducted. The publicly Jewish Silverman jokes: 'Everybody blames the Jews for killing Christ, and then the Jews try to pass it off on the Romans. I'm one of the few people that believe it was the blacks.' If you find the joke funny, it is both because it parodies the idea that entire ethnicities can be responsible for single events and because it recognises the primacy of racism against African-Americans in the US, even as it assumes that we don't believe that the 'real' Sarah Silverman actually believes this. The complexity of this explanation of course eradicates the humour from the joke but it shows the importance of comedy in and as democracy that I want to explore here before moving on to discuss specific aspects of *Seinfeld*'s humour in the next two chapters.

If the prominence of questions of ethnicity in American comedy in general from *All in the Family* to Chris Rock is at one level a displaced way of addressing the question of class, and on another level is always disavowed as 'just a joke', what happens to ethnicity itself? There were two related responses in the 1990s to this dilemma. On the one hand, performers began to make their personal identity the subject of their comedy. While there is no truly new subject for comedy, and there are always precedents, the expansion of comedy clubs, the rise of cable TV and the national debate over multiculturalism in the US gave this issue a new prominence. Performers like the Korean Margaret Cho made their backgrounds central to their work, laughing at it from a position of understanding as well as irritation. Cho also had a short-lived television series, *All-American Girl* (1994–5), that was one of the first to make Korean-Americans the central characters. As the title of Cho's series suggests, its central topic was the old issue of assimilation and integration versus staying true to diaspora traditions. This once-private debate within American minority cultures was now offered to a national audience as the subject for comedy, rather than angst. In an earlier generation, these questions had surfaced in television series like *The Goldbergs* (1948–56) at a time when relatively few people had access to television. By the same token, the dilemmas of immigration had been extensively debated in literature by writers like James Baldwin, Zora Neale Hurston, Saul Bellow and Philip Roth. All these writers could be comic, especially Roth, but their literary form restricted their audience. With its creation of the mass audience, television made such debates national and international.

71

At the same time, for all the discussion of what it was to be black in Chris Rock's work, or the intersection of Jewish and lesbian identity in Sandra Bernhard's performance work, one overweening question could not be addressed at this time. In the politics of 'race', the most explosive question is whether differences between people are or are not innate. With the success of scurrilous books like Richard J. Hernnstein and Charles Murray's *The Bell Curve* (1994) that claimed African-Americans were 'naturally' less intelligent than 'whites', such issues were alive in the culture at large in the 1990s.[18] Comedy displaced them again into questions of gender and sexuality, where it is perceived to be less dangerous to discuss innate differences. Popular books like *Men Are from Mars, Women Are from Venus* (1992) went so far as to claim that straight men and women were entirely different species. A great deal of stand-up comedy centred on the differences between men and women, whether at work, on the dating scene or in marriage. In 1990, the activist group Queer Nation put a new term into the popular vocabulary, when they tried to out the talk-show host Arsenio Hall from the audience of his show. It is interesting that they chose to out a television performer, and one with a mass, popular audience at that, rather than an artistic or political celebrity. In part, the nation that needed 'queering' was TV-land, which was officially straight at the time. Almost at once, a debate began between those who saw queer as the definition of a certain form of lesbian and gay identity, and thus a highly particular form of personal identity, and those for whom it suggested the blurring of classification by sexuality from the either/or of straight/gay into something more complicated. Discussions of the seemingly permanent differences between men and women were now undercut by the possibility that a person's lack of understanding of the other sex was motivated by the desire for their own.

72

While American political culture has responded to this as a threat, passing laws for the Defense of Marriage (1996) and other such absurdities, there was also a comic opportunity here. Jerry Seinfeld, who was often rumoured to be gay himself, was untroubled by the gossip and headed directly for the jokes. What was at stake in such highly charged debates were the rules by which a society ordered and arranged itself. How did one belong and by what right? Who was allowed to claim this belonging and who not? Who decided? What was appropriate behaviour both for those in the new identity groups and for those interacting with them? As I have suggested, these kinds of questions were central to *Seinfeld* and gave it the particular force that it had in the period. Without ever directly addressing politics in the traditional sense, *Seinfeld* worried at great length about the question of Jewish identity in the 1990s and at even greater length about sex and sexuality.

# 4 Too Jewish

When I lived in England, I was always too Jewish. At any time when
I had to mention my last name, I could depend on the question:
'Mirzoeff? That's not an English name is it?' At the same time, I was
aware of the irony that many of the key British television producers, like
my own father, who had done so much to shape the modern sense of
Englishness, were Jewish. I used to think that this was a personal
observation until I read in Martin Amis's autobiography *Experience*
(2000) that one of the ways in which his father, Kingsley Amis, would
indulge his avowed anti-Semitism was to scan the credits of BBC arts
programmes looking for Jewish names.[19] He would certainly have found
them. When I arrived in New York, I found that I was not Jewish
enough. A well-known art historian brought one dinner party to a halt
with her shout of disbelief that I was Jewish but did not know Yiddish.
By the same token, I found myself the rank outsider when I had to
confess that I had not been in therapy. So *Seinfeld*'s take on being Jewish
in New York was refreshingly different. It acknowledged the sensibility
of Jewishness without subscribing to nostalgia for a lost immigrant past
or paranoia about ubiquitous anti-Semitism. For many of those working
on the show, *Seinfeld* was original precisely in having a Jewish lead
character without either masking that Jewishness or making a special
plea for it. *Seinfeld*'s mode of being funny about Jewishness was
distinctly of its times – what I call 'Oslo-era Jewishness'. That is to say,
in the period in which the 1993 Oslo Peace Accord dominated
assumptions about the future of the Middle East, it was possible for the

first time since the nineteenth century to think of Jewishness outside the tension of diaspora and nation-state. More importantly, there were new ways to be funny about being Jewish without worrying about being 'too Jewish'. Since the second *intifada* began in 2000, followed by the election victory of Hamas in the Palestinian Authority and the Israeli invasion of Lebanon, such optimism has now disappeared.

Jews have been central to American television but Jewishness has not. By this I mean that, while many performers and film-makers have been Jewish, their work has tended not to deal directly with questions of Jewishness, even when Jews were represented directly.[20] In clubs and theatres, Jewish comedians like Lenny Bruce and Jackie Mason talked about little else but to an audience that was mostly Jewish or sufficiently urban to be familiar with what was being joked about. The first Jewish comedy on American television was the family-based comedy series the *The Goldbergs*. The Goldbergs were a recognisably Jewish family who moved in the course of the series from the New York tenements associated with nineteenth-century immigration to the Long Island suburbs, where both the real Jerry Seinfeld and his TV alter ego grew up. The NBC executive Brandon Tartikoff said in 1983 that *The Goldbergs* (or a show like it) 'would not work today. It worked when television was new, television sets expensive, and the owners were disproportionately Jewish.'[21] Tartikoff's suggestion was that *The Goldbergs* was possible because early television was in effect what we now call narrow-casting, reaching only a small portion of the population, comparable to the Internet in the early 1990s. Once television became a mass medium, in the mid-1950s, it followed that such shows would no longer be possible, at least in the view of the network executives, who then ensured that this was in fact the case. Indeed, Tartikoff responded to the pilot for *Seinfeld* with the comment 'Too New York, too Jewish' that gives this chapter its title.[22]

The comment 'too Jewish' is a part of internal Jewish discussions of identity, made from one Jew to another in regards to a gesture, a comment or a form of appearance. It is part of the defence mechanism of assimilation that has been summed up in the saying

'We're not men'

attributed to the eighteenth-century Jewish philosopher Moses Mendelssohn: 'Be a man on the outside and a Jew on the inside.' That is to say, assimilation required that outsiders be unable to detect your Jewishness that nonetheless remained intact inside. Both issues were of great concern to *Seinfeld*. As George and Jerry wait to meet NBC, George panics and says: 'These are men, Jerry. Men with jobs.' By contrast, as they agree later, 'We're not men' (episode 156, 'The Summer of George', 1997). Of course, as we shall discuss in the next chapter, this presentation of Jewishness as masculinity raises important questions about Jewish women. Here, these anxieties will be considered as anxieties about ethnicity.

As mentioned earlier, *Seinfeld* drew inspiration from the television version of *The Jack Benny Program*. Jack Benny's prominence meant that a Jew was the best-known television comedian of his day. It is usually said that Benny's programme did not have much to say about his Jewishness. In the episodes I have seen, there is nonetheless a constant harping on Benny's cheap ways with money. Benny's regular reminders to his audience of his Jewishness in this most stereotypical of ways should be seen as a pre-emptive defence against being attacked as a Jew. By making fun of his ethnicity himself, Benny effectively foreclosed the possibility that it could be used against him to such good result that people who saw the show do not remember any mention of Jewishness at all. One whole episode revolved around Benny keeping a dime given to him by Mary Livingston for over thirty years, while another made fun of the extremely elaborate security in his house. In the stand-up section at the end of one show, Benny claimed that there was talk of making a Hollywood movie about his life. He had nominated actors like Paul Newman to play himself but said that the studio was insisting on Jascha Heifetz (1900–87), the well-known Israeli violinist. While Benny's Jewish 'inside' was revealed in this constant insistence on his cheapness, his manly 'outside' was far from secure, perhaps because his Jewishness was too visible. He portrayed himself in a noticeably effeminate way, the subject of repeated jokes in the series. Benny made his character the target of the jokes so that, as he put it, 'the minute I come on, even the most hen-pecked guy in the audience feels good'.[23] This is a double-edged remark, putting himself down along with a generation of American men, iconically depicted by James Dean's father in *Rebel without a Cause* (1956) being seen wearing an apron (trivia point: the actress Liz Sheridan who plays Helen Seinfeld used to date Dean). At the same time, it was a noticeably misogynistic comment, relying on the stereotype of the nagging wife as the cause of masculine insecurities.

Throughout Jewish comedy there is a tension about the classification of ethnicity – and the resulting gender anxieties – that is a key source of its humour. *Seinfeld* frequently quotes the 1980 film *The Elephant Man*, starring John Hurt, especially its signature line 'Don't look at me! I'm horrible!'. The so-called Elephant Man was John Merrick, a person with disabilities rescued from life in a freak show by a doctor in nineteenth-century England. The American freak-show tradition relied on the question 'What is it?', as the P. T. Barnum circus put it. This popular spectacle ran from 1860 to 1924 and put a person of colour on display to answer the question, posed on a poster of the period: 'Is it a lower order of MAN? Or is it a higher order of 'MONKEY?'[24]. The history of popular entertainment and comedy cannot be divorced from these unpleasant aspects that continue to have resonances in the comedy of the present. As already mentioned, Kramer suggests to Jerry that his TV pilot should be about 'freaks' and later on he has an altercation with a monkey (episode 109, 'The Face Painter', 1995). When the monkey spits at him, Kramer throws a banana peel back, causing the monkey to become so depressed that he 'curtails his autoerotic activities' to quote the zoo keeper. Kramer is forced to apologise to the monkey, which then resumes its attack on him. This sequence is certainly funny. Like many such moments in *Seinfeld* and other Jewish comedy, its humour is based on a form of anxiety that resolves into laughter, as in the expression 'nervous laughter'.

　　　The classic representation of this form of anxiety is the scene in Woody Allen's 1976 film *Annie Hall* in which Allen is having dinner with Annie's very WASP family in New England and the camera pans round to see him dressed as a Hasidic Jew complete with long beard and Homburg hat. The camera represents here the way that Allen feels himself to be looked at by the Halls. An internal pun refers to the black hat, coat, beard and glasses worn as a 'Jewish' costume by vaudeville performers. By being looked at, he feels transformed. In a closely contemporary essay, film theorist Laura Mulvey had famously argued that the cinematic gaze was male, rendering men the active lookers and women the looked-at. Allen added a twist, in that the gaze could also be Gentile (or white in general), an order of looking that, as it were, trumps Allen's masculinity by asserting a racialised superiority. I used to refer to this scene when giving talks at universities or colleges in places like New England. Often the remark would be greeted with wholly disproportionate laughter, which I came to see as a displacement of the fact that the audience had already recognised that I was Jewish and could now laugh off their anxiety at having made this identification. Now some people will read this and think, 'How paranoid', while others will perhaps identify similar moments in their own experience. It's that gap between paranoia and identification that is the source of what has become known as 'Jewish humour'.

Paranoia was understood by Freud to be a projection of something of which one is afraid or concerned about outside the body. In terms of Mendelssohn's dichotomy, it would be the question of being a 'man'. Identification is the opposite: the taking of something or someone from outside into the self, as it were, as a point of reference. In this instance, that would be the question of being Jewish. So when George does 'the opposite' (episode 86, 1994), he projects his Jewish self, angst and all, into the world, rather than the version of being a man that he has tried to put together up until that point. When he begins a conversation with the woman who subsequently becomes his girlfriend, instead of claiming to be an architect or a marine biologist as he usually does with disastrous results, he says instead: 'My name is George. I'm unemployed and live with my parents.' Rather than the expected ridicule, George is suddenly found intriguing. In the terms derived from Aristotle that I suggested in the last chapter, *Seinfeld* makes its comedy out of the ridicule directed at Jews and the ridiculousness of being Jewish.

*Seinfeld* reworked Jewish humour for its own time, rejecting earlier Jewish comedies like *The Goldbergs* or the Mary Tyler Moore spin-off *Rhoda* (1974–8) as being out of date, while looking askance at its contemporaries such as *Mad about You* (1992–9) and *Friends* for not engaging with the lead characters' Jewishness. One of the first episodes of the series (episode 7, 'The Pony Remark', 1991) made *Seinfeld*'s interest in Jewish issues central to its plot. The story revolves around a fiftieth wedding anniversary party for his cousin Manya that Jerry is forced to attend by his parents, visiting from Florida. He finds himself at a long dining table surrounded by older people, and, like many young people in such situations, becomes too loud and tries too hard to be funny. He does a routine about hating people who had ponies when they were children, only to provoke an angry response from Manya. It turns out she had a pony in her apparently idyllic childhood in Poland, where

'*I had a pony!*'                    The Pony Remark

all her friends and relatives had had ponies. To rub in the
embarrassment, it is revealed that she was actually from Krakow, the
nearest town to the concentration camps at Auschwitz-Birkenau, where
the country is in fact filled with grassy meadows. Further, if Manya and
Isaac had been married for fifty years, they would have been married in
1941 during World War II. Following the shock of these combined
memories she leaves the table and sinks into a rapid decline that leads to
her death. Although Jerry has now been responsible for the demise of a
Holocaust survivor, he still wants to skip the funeral for his
championship softball game. Even Elaine and George agree that he
cannot possibly miss the funeral and Elaine goes herself, admittedly in
the hope of renting the deceased's apartment.

79

When it rains during the funeral, the game is postponed and
Jerry thinks that his doing the right thing has been vindicated. But in the
replay, Jerry's terrible play costs his team the game, attributed by all to
the vengeful spirit of Manya. This show was one of the first to become a
'classic' *Seinfeld* and it is often cited by Jerry Seinfeld and Larry David as
an important step. However, you would have had to watch very
carefully to realise what was going on. Mixed in with Elaine's pursuit of
a dead person's apartment and George's Woody Allen-esque declaration

George in despair as usual

that there is no way he will ever have sex again, Manya's Polish origins
are mentioned in an aside and no one makes the deduction that her
marriage would have been during the war. Even at the level of
implication and deduction, the idea of making Jewish experience in
World War II the subject of humour was a daring step, one that might
not be possible now, as we shall see. Even the casual viewer, though,
could clearly see that *Seinfeld* was invested in a generational divide
between those who were either immigrants or the children of
immigrants and those who thought of themselves as simply American.
It was a new humour that no longer knew its *schlemiel* from its
*schlimazel* (two targets of Yiddish jokes).[25]

     The next episode that dealt directly with Jewish issues was not
broadcast until 14 October 1993, coincidentally just a month after the
signing of the Oslo Declaration of Principles, better known as the Oslo
Peace Accord, in Washington, DC. In Bill Clinton's autobiography, he
revealed that the behind-the-scenes activity on that day had centred on a

very *Seinfeld*-esque piece of business, namely how to prevent Yasser Arafat, leader of the Palestinian Liberation Organisation, from kissing the Israeli Prime Minister Yitzhak Rabin, as is the Arab custom.[26] Rabin was prepared to shake hands but would not submit to being kissed by his old enemy. Clinton and his National Security Adviser Tony Lake practised a form of handshake involving a grip on the left elbow that would prevent Arafat from 'moving in', as Clinton put it. Later in *Seinfeld*, an entire episode was devoted to the prevalence of 'The Kiss Hello' (episode 103, 1995), in which Jerry is ostracised in his own building for refusing to be kissed. In Clinton's case, the anti-kiss manoeuvre was successful. It turns out that this seemingly comic episode had a serious and negative side. Clinton describes how Rabin intended his 'body language' to display to the conservative side of his audience in Israel his lack of conviction about the new agreement. Such triangulation was the basis of Clinton's politics and its costs have become clear as time goes on, not least with the assassination of Yitzhak Rabin on 4 November 1995 and the subsequent collapse of any chance for peace in the Middle East.

81

It did not appear so at the time. Although some, like the far-sighted critic Edward Said, criticised the Oslo declaration from the first, for many it seemed like a genuinely hopeful development. By offering the chance of a resolution of forty years of conflict, the declaration also suggested that it might now be possible to imagine a new way to be Jewish, one that was less beholden to the ghosts and anxieties of the past and more open to the issues of its own time. In 'The Bris' (episode 69, 1993), *Seinfeld* began to take such a new approach, beginning with the fundamental issue of the covenant between Israel (meaning the Jews) and God as marked by male circumcision, the *bris* of the title. Although the episode was careful to explain its terminology to the audience, it was a strikingly 'Jewish' subject for American television, just the kind of thing that would have been thought of as 'too Jewish' in earlier periods. As godparents to the new-born child of their friends, Jerry and Elaine have to arrange a *bris* for the boy but, although they know what needs to be done, they have no idea how to do it. Elaine has to look up *mohel* (the circumciser) in the telephone directory, prompting Jerry to make fun of her journey from 'finishing school' to *mohel* even as he agitates about having to hold the infant during the procedure. So is Elaine Jewish? Who knows? The task prompts them to discuss whether they have seen an uncircumcised man. Jerry has not, while Elaine did see one once, the memory of which causes her to screw up her face in disgust and shake her head. For once, the intensely verbal comedy is at a loss for words. She recovers to declare the offending organ lacked 'personality'. While male circumcision was more or less standard for children born in the United States between 1945 and 1980, this sense of the uncircumcised as being alien is a noticeable marker of difference. The ceremony organised by Jerry and Elaine is a predictable disaster, with Kramer intervening to protect the baby from the 'barbaric' custom, George fainting away at the prospect and Jerry getting his finger cut by the nervous and agitated *mohel*. By making fun of first the Holocaust, albeit implicitly, and then circumcision, *Seinfeld* took the most sacred cows of American Jewish life and made them available for comedy.

82

At the end of 'The Bris', the parents remove godparental status from Jerry and Elaine and bestow it on Kramer. The scene is set up as a parody of Francis Ford Coppola's classic film *The Godfather* (1972). As we have seen, *Seinfeld* shows often end on this form of visual pun in which a television programme suddenly assumes the aura of the Hollywood film. Here Jerry Seinfeld's insistence on shooting the programme on film was justified, as it gave the parody visual force. Now at one level this is just a bit of playful humour. But it is worth thinking about why such a simple gag is so funny. Hollywood cinema is America's great cultural achievement, creating a range of emotional, visual and linguistic references that is more than simply American, becoming the cultural expression of globalisation. I remember walking in Los Angeles on my first day there and, despite the jet lag, I felt very much at home because the light and space were so familiar to me from countless films and television programmes made in Southern California. It is in this sense that even those places most hostile to the United States' foreign policy will often have a strong appreciation for its films, music and popular culture. By taking the old-world tradition of the *bris*, done at home by a *mohel* in Orthodox fashion, and having it lead to a cinematic conclusion, *Seinfeld* turned being Jewish into a variant of being American in the classic assimilationist fashion. What the (television) Jews aspire to here is not just being American but being in the movies.

Ironically, Hollywood was originally the creation of Jews from Warner Bros. to Metro-Goldwyn-Mayer.[27] Like television after it, Hollywood had at first made films that directly addressed the Jewish audience, like *The Jazz Singer* (1927), the first talkie. The film tells the story of how Jackie Rabinowitz, played by Al Jolson, the son of a cantor, or singer, in a synagogue, becomes Jack Robin, a theatrical minstrel star in blackface. His song 'Mammie' performed as a minstrel is the high point of the film, complete with a soundtrack. But when his father falls ill, he returns home to sing the Kol Nidre, one of the most important parts of the service on Yom Kippur. While Jolson's generation became American by pretending to be African-American, *Seinfeld*'s pretended to be Italians, both Catholics and gangsters. Perhaps, as many have complained in the wake of *The Sopranos* (1999–2007), the cliché Italian gangster is the last ethnic stereotype that is acceptable in contemporary American media. Again, as Lenny Bruce used to have it, in the division of the world into Jewish and goyish, the Italians are Jewish. But in *Seinfeld*, assimilation is a joke in which the Jews become Italian by means of the cinema. Jewishness loses its intense specificity, taken by friends and enemies alike to be marked by circumcision, and becomes just another way to be American. It made *Seinfeld* sufficiently generic that it could be accepted in America, though the Jewish aspects of its humour may have accounted for its marginal popularity in the UK. It is usually said that *Seinfeld* failed in the UK because it was scheduled in unpopular late-night slots, but the paranoid Jewish response is, of course, '*Why* do you think it got bad times? Because it was too Jewish!'

Be that as it may, empowered by this 'Oslo-era Jewishness', *Seinfeld* next returned to the Holocaust through cinema, specifically

83

Stephen Spielberg's 1993 film *Schindler's List*. Oddly there was a certain symbiosis between *Seinfeld* and *Schindler's List*. Spielberg reportedly had new episodes of *Seinfeld* flown out for the cast to watch, presumably as a relief from the stress of re-enacting the Holocaust. The cinematic release of *Schindler's List* then came to play a role in *Seinfeld*'s reworking of American Jewishness. As I suggested in Chapter 1, *Seinfeld* is about nothing precisely because it worried about approaching serious issues such as the Holocaust at anything less than epic length. *Schindler* served as a shorthand reference that could encompass both the moral gravity of being Jewish and the artistic difficulty of representing it. In a two-part episode (episodes 82–3, 'The Raincoats, parts 1 and 2', 1994), Jerry's parents are staying with him in his apartment. His current girlfriend Rachel Goldstein – the only identifiably Jewish girlfriend of his long list of fictional amours – is also living with her parents, so a certain frustration sets in, as the Seinfelds delay their departure for a European holiday to make a deal selling vintage raincoats with Kramer. Jerry's parents insist that he must go to see *Schindler's List* – implicitly, seeing the film became a moral requirement of being Jewish. The mailman Newman (Wayne Knight), described by Jerry as 'pure evil', spies Jerry making out with Rachel throughout the film and takes advantage of the opportunity to tell Jerry's parents what he saw. Not only does Jerry face the hostility of his own parents, for the only time in the series, but Rachel's father, a rabbi, ends their relationship. This episode suggests that being Jewish is perceived as a constraint from childhood, like a curfew, that can safely be made fun of as adults. In the final scene, Elaine's boyfriend Aaron (the close talker), who has unaccountably been taking the elder Seinfelds to all manner of New York attractions, breaks down as Jerry's parents finally board their plane. In what is now clearly a parody of *Schindler*, he suggests he could have done more for them and when Elaine demurs, he points to his wrist and says: 'This watch! I could have sold this watch! This ring is one more dinner I could have taken them out to!'. This parodies the end of the film when Oskar Schindler (Liam Neeson) has a similar fit of grief, suggesting that he could have sold his ring to save one

84

more person. There was just a very faint hint of the ridiculous here that *Seinfeld* homed in on with great daring. Aaron hurtles towards the gate, insisting that the Seinfelds must have water, echoing the scene in Spielberg's film where Schindler forces the SS to spray water on a train full of Jews on a hot day. Although a particularly sensitive person might see this as making fun of the Holocaust, what *Seinfeld* was actually doing was parodying a film and the show attracted no controversy.

This strategy of handling Jewishness in relationship to other media or other religions seemed to work and *Seinfeld* stuck with it. For example, when Jerry makes fun of his Uncle Leo for suggesting that his hamburger was overdone because the cook was anti-Semitic, he does so to a national audience on *The Tonight Show* (episode 126, 'The Shower Head', 1996). The dentist Tim Whatley converts to Judaism but Jerry suspects that he has done it not out of any principle but for the jokes (episode 153, 'The Yada Yada', 1997). He complains to Whatley's priest in the Catholic confessional and the priest asks whether this offends him as a Jewish person, to which Jerry replies, 'No, it offends me as a comedian.' The joke makes fun of a certain presumption of what one might call identity comedy: in order to make fun of a given ethnicity, sexuality or religion, it must be one you directly identify with. That sense of direct identification 'as' a Jew becomes the target of the joke here. At the same time, the episode makes fun of people's need to have an identity that is distinctively theirs in a culture that is irreversibly mixed. Finally, it was refreshing to hear the idea that it might be desirable to be Jewish, not because of the Jews' exemplary suffering, but because they had the best jokes. I'd rather be in the funniest minority than the one that suffered the most.

As if tired of being told to adhere to certain ways of being 'because you're Jewish', the humour in *Seinfeld* was more than willing to play with the all-important 1990s' category of identity. In a fifth season episode called 'The Conversion' (episode 75, 1993), George decides to convert to Latvian Orthodox Christianity in order to impress a woman who has ended a relationship with him because he was not of this faith (which does in fact exist, and was very grateful for the

85

promotion). Although the conversion involves a lengthy theological test, George cheats by writing the answers on his hand and passes with flying colours. So, as he announces, he is set to become Brother Costanza. 'And what', asks Jerry, 'is Brother Costanza planning on telling Mother Costanza?'. Brother Costanza's promised 'vow of silence' is undone when Estelle discovers his plan through a friend. A volcanic scene ensues among the Costanza family, reminiscent of what happens when Woody Allen tells his mother in *Hannah and Her Sisters* (1986) that he is converting to Catholicism. During the filming, Estelle Harris asked Larry David if her character was Jewish. His response was 'What do you care?'. In David's view, what matters is getting the laugh, not continuity of character. His approach runs contrary to the dominant Method school of acting in the US in which the actor attempts to perform as if she or he is really experiencing their character's life and emotions. Meryl Streep's legendary efforts to learn Polish for her role as Sophie Zawistowstka in *Sophie's Choice* (1982), or the violin for *Music of the Heart* (1999) are the epitome of this approach. *Seinfeld* was less than impressed – 'Oh that Meryl Streep, she's such a phoney' was Jerry's line, while in similar vein Elaine was physically unable to stand watching the Anthony Minghella film *The English Patient* (1996) because of its 'phoney' seriousness (episode 151, 'The English Patient', 1997). David espouses the alternative view of theatre promoted by Bertolt Brecht that the audience should not be made to identify with the characters but rather to feel alienated from them. In his own series *Curb Your Enthusiasm* – whose very title invites the audience not to enjoy the show – this connection is signalled by the use of incidental music from Brecht and Weill's musical *The Happy End* (1929).

In this vein, it follows that George is sometimes Jewish and sometimes Italian, perhaps being from a mixed marriage. While Estelle Costanza refuses to drive a German car, a typically New York Jewish position (episode 146, 'The Money', 1997), Frank Costanza reminisces about his Italian relatives. Nothing is ever clarified, because it was not a priority. When George gets engaged, Elaine confides her feelings of jealousy to a rabbi. Unfortunately the rabbi has a cable TV show and broadcasts her views to the world, using the real names of the people involved. In this episode, it is clear that Elaine is not Jewish, both because she says as much to the rabbi and because Jerry offers to explain the ways of the Jewish people to her (episode 112, 'The Postponement', 1995). With Elaine's identity newly decided, she has to fend off her 'shiksappeal' to a series of Jewish men and boys. A 'shiksa' is a Yiddish term for a Gentile woman and there is also a pun on the idea of sex appeal. The joke here was double-edged because the actress Julia Louis-Dreyfus, who played Elaine, is Jewish, as was certainly well known to fans by the ninth series. Adam, the son of her long-time boss Mr Lippman (Richard Fancy), kisses her at his bar mitzvah (the coming-of-age ceremony for thirteen-year-old Jewish boys). When she goes to the Lippman house to smooth things over, Adam asks her on a date, which she declines because he is still a boy. Adam renounces Judaism on the spot, feeling that the bar-mitzvah ceremony in which he was proclaimed a man was nothing but a sham. Elaine then finds herself the subject of Mr Lippman's attentions and even those of the rabbi she turns to for help (episode 159, 'The Serenity Now', 1997). For all the silliness of this chain of desire, there is a definite anxiety in Jewish circles that Jewish men prefer shiksas, just as Spike Lee's film *Jungle Fever* (1991) explored the preference among some African-American men for white women. To deal with such issues in public, as opposed to within the community, is often seen as problematic. In the case of Jews, all such behaviour is often explained using the blanket pop psychology of self-hatred – that is to say, you date Gentiles because you hate the Jewish part of yourself. Rather than see Elaine's role reversal as self-hating, it seems to me to suggest a willingness to explore some of the contradictions of Jewishness through a humour that does not demand identification with a certain way of being Jewish.

87

Of course, if you're looking for humiliation and embarrassment, who better to turn to than your family? Jerry's family problems begin with the basic greeting, as epitomised by his Uncle Leo's (Len Lesser) theatrical 'Hello!'. On the way to revive their proposed pilot at NBC, George and Jerry have to break short the extended family greeting ritual with Uncle Leo, causing inevitable offence. Jerry spends the moments before the crucial meeting obsessing over how this is going to reverberate around the family, as indeed it does. As in all immigrant communities, Jewish family life is a tension between being close and being suffocated. Money is often the symbol of this drama. When his mother insists on sending him $50 when he bounces a cheque, Jerry is incensed. On the other hand, when he gives a Cadillac to his father in the self-conscious effort to be a 'good son', it backfires completely (episodes 124–5, 'The Cadillac, parts 1 and 2', 1996). Jerry's father, Morty (Barney Martin), is President of the board of Del Boca Vista, his Florida retirement housing complex. The other board members, led by the resentful Jack Kloppus (Sandy Baron), conclude that the Cadillac was purchased with money embezelled from the apartment complex and they impeach Morty. The explanation that Jerry bought the car is dismissed as impossible: 'We all saw his act.' So financial, professional and personal humiliation are mixed in a way that only a family could produce, only a Jewish family at that.

As the expression of a new generation of Jewishness, *Seinfeld*'s take on Jewish humour gained considerable traction within the community. In 1996, the Jewish Museum in New York staged an exhibition under the title 'Too Jewish?'. Curated by Norman L. Kleeblatt, the exhibition mostly showed parodic and self-reflexive works of art, such as Deborah Kass's *4 Barbras* (Jackie Series, 1992), a parody of Andy Warhol's famous screen prints that took Barbra Streisand as its icon, rather than Jackie Kennedy or Marilyn Monroe. The work is funny but it also makes a claim for the inclusion of Jewish icons, like Streisand, within the American canon of heroes and heroines. The exhibition also found space for television shows that concerned Jews and Jewishness, including *Seinfeld*. In fact, 'The Bris' (episode 69, 1993) is now part of the museum's permanent collection. After 9/11 and the collapse of the Middle East peace process, such nuance is no longer available. In 2002, Kleeblatt again tried to move Jewish views forward in his exhibition 'Mirroring Evil', which brought together a series of artworks that dealt with the Nazi perpetrators of evil. A number of the works used parody and humour, such as Zbigniew Libera's work *Lego Concentration Camp* (1996). As the title suggests, the Polish artist had imagined how a Lego set might be made of the Auschwitz concentration camp, following the suggestion by many scholars of the Holocaust that the camps were in fact an appalling but logical corollary of the capitalist production process.[28] This exhibition was greeted with utter outrage, leading to pickets by Holocaust survivors and death threats to some of the organisers. The mediated approach to the Holocaust was no longer acceptable in an era that thinks of the world as neatly divided into good and evil.

In his HBO series *Curb Your Enthusiasm*, *Seinfeld* co-producer Larry David has recently returned to such questions with a sharper edge. On the one hand, the themes have become more pronouncedly Jewish, but on the other, the humour is far more aggressive. *Curb Your Enthusiasm* works as the alter *Seinfeld*. Like *Seinfeld*, *Curb* deals with the fictional everyday life of its creator, in this case Larry David. While *Seinfeld* was a New York show, *Curb* is set in Los Angeles, and the privileged entertainment high-life Los Angeles at that. In *Seinfeld*, the characters go to a coffee shop but in *Curb*, Larry David and his friends buy a restaurant. Whereas *Seinfeld* was very tightly scripted and edited, *Curb* is an improvisational show in which the actors work around a scene outline without scripted dialogue. The shooting is on video and has no aspirations to be cinematic. The humour revolves around the extraordinarily embarrassing situations the fictional Larry David gets himself into, with the result that it is not always possible to find them funny on first viewing. In this regard, *Curb* is reminiscent of the British classic *Fawlty Towers* (1975–9), in which John Cleese played right on the boundaries of humour and offensiveness. The 2005 season of *Curb* had a story arc about the fictional Larry David's exploration of his family background and thereby his Jewishness. In episode 1 ('The Larry David Sandwich'), David buys a ticket to a Rosh Hashanah (New Year) service in synagogue from a scalper (tout) and when he gets found out, he is ejected by security. The joke revolves around the fact that seats in synagogue are sold on a yearly basis, a typically uncomfortable 'inside' detail of Jewishness as in *Seinfeld*. In *Curb*, the question is dealt with head-on as part of Judaism not Jewishness, without mediation through cinema or comparison with other religions. Later in the series, David develops an elaborate ruse in which he pretends to be Orthodox to try to get his friend Richard Lewis bumped up the kidney donor list by an organ supplier, who happens to be Orthodox (season 5, episode 5, 'Lewis Needs a Kidney'). David takes the organ supplier on a ski-trip, during which he presents his friend Jeff's wife Susie (Susie Essmann) as his own, presumably because his real wife, Cheryl (Cheryl Hines), is either not Jewish, or not Jewish enough, being blonde and blue-eyed. Inevitably, the deception is uncovered and Lewis does not get the kidney. So from *Seinfeld*'s play with the idea of being 'too Jewish', Larry David has now reverted to a position where the comedy derives from not being Jewish enough.

While such explorations of identity are acceptable on cable, since the collapse of the peace process Jews and Jewishness have disappeared from network television, giving way to more or less explicitly Christian programming from *Touched by an Angel* (1994–2003) to *Joan of Arcadia* (2003–5). Now even the ability to laugh at Jewish jokes has been suspended. The preposterous character Borat on Sacha Baron-Cohen's *Da Ali G Show* (2000, UK; 2003–4, UK/US) made a series of trips to America in the series shown on HBO in 2004. He performs at a country-and-western venue what he claims to be a 'Kazakh children's song' with the title 'Throw the Jew Down the Well (So My Country Can Be Free)'. Borat quickly wins over his audience and by the end of his song even the one woman who had at first looked a little shocked was singing along and clapping in time. First and foremost, this depiction of Borat's antics is hilarious, because it makes ridiculous two unappealing characteristics of his participants: first, some people will do absolutely anything to be on TV, as the wilder reaches of reality TV are amply demonstrating; and second, anti-Semitism is at best tolerated and at worst still active in some parts of the American South. By making visible what is already there, Borat makes it ridiculous, because such prejudices now rely on being unspoken except in private. Nonetheless, the Anti-Defamation League immediately protested against the song, seemingly failing to realise that someone called Cohen might actually be Jewish – oh, I forgot, he must be a *self-hating* Jew. Interestingly, Cohen turned to a former *Seinfeld* writer Larry Charles to be the director for his 2006 movie *Borat: Cultural Learnings of America for Make Benefit of Glorious Nation Kazakhstan* that once again reworks anti-Semitic stereotypes through the mouthpiece of his naive character. Inevitably, the success of the film in the US provoked a large number of opinion pieces claiming that this type of humour was unacceptable.

At the same time, the singular sense of identity claimed by post-Holocaust Jews in general, and Oslo-era Jewishness in particular, led to the most obvious failure of *Seinfeld*, namely its depiction of an almost all-white Manhattan. When people of colour appear at all, they

91

Ping, the Chinese delivery person

are usually restaurant staff or in sports. The only recurring characters of colour were Ping, a Chinese restaurant delivery person; Mr Morgan, an African-American who works for the New York Yankees with George; and the Johnny-Cochrane-parody-lawyer Jackie Chiles. Although many white Americans do live in homogenous social circles, it is very unlikely that the four characters would have spent a decade in New York without meeting more professional people of colour. If this point seems a little humourless, it was widespread at the time the series was going out and was directed at *Seinfeld*'s primary claim to reflect everyday life. One of the hallmarks of everyday life in New York is precisely its diversity and it is one of the pleasures of the city. In response to such criticism, *Seinfeld* held its own ethnic stereotyping up to ridicule when Jerry presents a cigar-store Indian to Elaine in front of her Native American friend Winona (episode 74, 'The Cigar Store Indian', 1993). Unaware of her background, he makes a ridiculous speech in fake 'Indian' talk as popularised by Westerns – 'we smoke um peace-pipe', for example. Very embarrassed to discover the situation, Jerry goes to Winona's apartment to apologise. He offers to take her for a Szechuan meal to make up and asks the mailman for directions. Unfortunately the postal worker turns out to be Chinese and furiously asks why he must know where the Chinese restaurants are? Jerry's explanation that he expected him to know because of his work, not his ethnicity, is undercut when Kramer drives by in a cab with the cigar-store Indian, making an 'Indian war whoop'. In these sequences, Jerry certainly looks ridiculous but the humour does not manage to find a way to get past the embarrassment by providing a take on white presumptions that would offer a catharsis of the ridiculous. By way of contrast, when the script for 'The Outing' (episode 57, 1993), in which George and Jerry are 'outed' as a gay couple, was first read by the cast, it was not found funny because it seemed to say that there was something wrong in being gay. In the rewriting process, the now-legendary catchphrase 'not that there's anything wrong with that' was added and turned a potentially offensive episode into a Gay and Lesbian Anti-Defamation Award winner. The phrase both made fun of a certain form of politicised everyday speech and highlighted the anxiety that straight people have around out gays and lesbians, while still managing to say what needed to be said about continuing prejudices. No similar device was found for negotiating white privilege.

*Seinfeld* did manage to expose to ridicule some of the contradictions of white life in New York, where schools in 2005 were found to be more segregated than they had been before the landmark 1954 *Brown v. Board of Education* Supreme Court case supposedly desegregated American education. In 'The Chinese Woman' (episode 90, 1994), Jerry's girlfriend of the week, Donna Chang, persuades Estelle not to divorce her husband Frank, much to George's relief. But at the dinner to celebrate, Estelle revokes her decision when she discovers that, despite her name, Donna is a 'white girl from Long Island'. Although Donna's advice had contained quotations from Confucius, these were no longer found compelling when not spoken by an authentically Chinese person. Here the Western cliché of ancient Chinese wisdom is exposed as a racialised prejudice in a way that is both comic and effective. As if trying to address the way in which *Seinfeld* had no characters of colour, George is forced to try and befriend Jerry's African-American exterminator in order to prove to Mr Morgan that he does have at least one friend of colour (episode 108, 'The Diplomat's Club', 1995). What undercuts the force of these exposures is that both take place within the barely sane parameters of the Costanza family, meaning that no one is likely to have derived any wider consequence from them. If George is a stand-in for Larry David, it would seem that these problems have continued to haunt *Curb Your Enthusiasm*. In the episode 'Affirmative Action' (episode 9, 2000), David makes a failed joke about affirmative action that has disastrous consequences. The problem is that, whatever you think of affirmative action, Larry's joke just wasn't very funny and therefore wasn't worth all the agonising.

These problems were recently thrown into dramatic relief by the scandal caused by Michael Richards's racist response to some African-American hecklers during his set at a Los Angeles comedy club in November 2006. While the comments made by the hecklers have not

been recorded, a video of Richards's response made by a patron using a
cell-phone camera circulated widely. He used a quite extraordinarily
violent degree of racist comment, suggesting that fifty years ago his
heckler would have been lynched for speaking back to a white person.
When the hecklers exclaimed that this was 'uncalled for', a rather
moderate retort under the circumstances, Richards exploded into a
stream of epithets. He called out 'Look, a nigger', in an unintended echo
of Frantz Fanon's famous analysis of a French child saying 'Look, a
negro!'.[29] One of the oddities of Richards's remarks was how
anachronistic they were. The last notorious lynching incidents were fifty
years ago, when Richards was a child, and he may have been repeating
some forgotten remark that he had overheard then under the stress of
performance. When he was ushered onto *The Late Show with David
Letterman* (1993–) by Jerry Seinfeld in order to apologise, Richards

Jerry and Kramer in
a happier moment

compounded his situation by referring repeatedly to 'Afro-Americans' and to 'blacks' as if it were still the 1960s. While Richards himself was not connected to the writing of *Seinfeld*, and his disastrous remarks do not necessarily invalidate a comedy that went off the air eight years earlier, there is no doubt that this incident casts the problematic place of race in *Seinfeld* into still greater relief.

Perhaps it is scarcely surprising that a sitcom like *Seinfeld* was not able to unpick the structures of American racialisation. My intent here is not to be overly censorious, or to score easy political-correctness points. The criticisms were made at the time the series was broadcast because the show was so aware of its time in other ways that this issue stood out. If this is *Seinfeld*'s most obvious failure, it was also that of Oslo-era Jewishness in general. In a sense, Jewish identity of the time felt protected from all accusations of bias by its legacy of terrible suffering and the new sense that peace was coming to the Middle East. When Jerry is trying to convince George that asking the mailman for directions to a Chinese restaurant is not racist, he claims: 'If someone asks me which way is Israel, I don't fly off the handle!'. The silliness of the idea makes it funny at the same time as showing a new confidence about introducing Israel into a joke. The underlying assumption here is the New York aphorism 'Whaddya want from me?'. In other words, simply being Jewish is supposed to be cast-iron proof that you are not racist and therefore you have no need to make gestures like casting actors because they happen to be African-American or Asian. Nonetheless, as the recurring incidents trying to deal with the question of ethnicity show, *Seinfeld* was aware of the problem it had set for itself and failed to resolve. Paradoxically, this very failure gave impetus to the area of its greatest success in the discussion of sex, sexuality and relationships. Here the writers could find a way to be funny about supposedly ingrained differences between people without crossing the fine line between daring and offensiveness. Not that there's anything wrong with that.

95

# **5** Not That There's Anything Wrong with That

If *Seinfeld* was ever about anything, as opposed to being about nothing, it was about relationships. As a show whose priority was making comedy, it was more precisely about how and why relationships fail to work. More precisely still, it was about the manifest and manifold failings of mainstream heterosexuality. The very fact that George can plausibly have a series of dates and eventually be engaged to someone like Susan suggests that the dating scene in New York has its problems. It is axiomatic in the city that there are no nice (straight) men to date – the phrase 'all the good ones are married or gay' echoes around the media commentary on the issue. Certainly, Elaine's experience on the show would reinforce that theme. *Seinfeld*'s era was one in which President Clinton's time in office seemed to hinge on his definition of sexual relations as a rather sad and unfulfilled experience. *Seinfeld* made comedy out of sexuality by being euphemistic, inarticulate and insinuating about it, allowing for a comic range of (mis)understandings. The deceptive ambivalence about Jewishness that was discussed in the last chapter – being a 'Jew' on the inside and a 'man' on the outside – played itself out as a sexuality that never knew what it really was. It projected heterosexuality to the outside world, while worrying constantly about what was really within. Certain only that they were not properly men, George and Jerry undertook excellent dating adventures in ways that made the implicit queerness of Jewish humour explicit for the first time.

Susan cracks up at the idea of a pre-nup

97

For all his anxieties, Woody Allen was always clear about being straight. But *Seinfeld* saw the dilemma of Jewishness for what it was: if being a 'man' is what you project out in paranoia, what is it in terms of gender and sexuality that you identify with within yourself?

Perhaps even before the question of straight relationships, *Seinfeld* was concerned with the question of relationships between men and where the boundaries were located between friendship and same-sex desire. This is not to say that *Seinfeld* was a 'gay' show, whatever that would mean, or that the characters were 'really' gay but that its humour relied on a series of uncertainties in an area that American culture likes to think of as absolutely determined. So while same-sex desire and even transgender have slowly become more acceptable in mainstream media culture on the grounds that this is how people 'really' are, bisexuality, gender queer and other more ambivalent modes of sexuality have continued to draw suspicion. As one of the characters on Showtime's hit *The L Word* (2004–) (in which L stands for Lesbian rather than Liberal) scornfully remarks: 'Bisexuals – make up your mind already!'. The use of the Jewish New York slang in a Los Angeles-based show is striking, suggesting a certain affinity between being Jewish and gender/sexuality vague. In her 1964 essay 'Notes on Camp', the quintessential New York intellectual Susan Sontag had signalled that affinity as what she called an 'analogy', one that was

> not frivolously chosen. Jews and homosexuals are the outstanding creative minorities in contemporary urban culture. Creative, that is, in the truest sense: they are creators of sensibilities. The two pioneering forces of modern sensibility are Jewish moral seriousness and homosexual aestheticism and irony.[30]

*Seinfeld* had signalled its seriousness by choosing to be about nothing, while finding itself strongly drawn to the irony of camp, if not its aestheticism. When Sontag calls camp a comedy drawn from the 'experience of underinvolvement, of detachment', we recognise *Seinfeld* at once. So too its taste for corny movies like *Plan 9 from Outer Space,* its attraction to outré statements of femininity like those of Bette Midler and Raquel Welsh, even the use of operas like *I Pagliacci* and *The Barber of Seville* for plot devices: all these *Seinfeld* tropes are camp. Yet the passion and the aestheticism of camp, even if ironic, seem a step too far for *Seinfeld* with its perpetual anxiety that camp Jewish irony might be taken for homosexuality or might even be homosexuality.

In the pilot episode *The Seinfeld Chronicles*, George (in his clever, anxious persona before he becomes the opposite) tells Jerry that relationships are all about 'signals', verbal, visual and physical. For instance, if someone says they *have* to be in town and *might* see you, they don't intend to do so. The extent of physical contact at greeting indicates what level your relationship has attained, except when a blindfold followed by a double-handshake is proffered – 'not in the playbook'. Despite this apparently sophisticated awareness, the characters in *Seinfeld* are terrible at reading signals and are often baffled by how to send them. To be fair, signals in America are very odd. Here

98

you can guarantee that the 'express' checkout in a supermarket will be the slowest, the passing (overtaking) lane on a freeway is always jammed with would-be speedsters, the directions to New York's airports are indicated by minute white-on-green pictures of aeroplanes and so on. If traffic is this much of a problem, is it any wonder that gender signals are so off these days? One of the first episodes of *Seinfeld* was called 'Male Unbonding' (episode 4, 1990) and concerned Jerry's futile efforts to separate from a male friend. While there are ways to break off a relationship, how does one break off a friendship? Although he tries the 'It's not you, it's me' routine, Joel, the friend in question, starts crying – 'there was mucus' – and Jerry can't go through with it. Later in the series, Jerry has to jump off a subway to evade a new male acquaintance trying to make friends with him because 'he has enough friends already' (episode 188, 'The Pool Guy', 1995). In another early episode called 'The Jacket' (episode 8, 1991), George gives a perfect demonstration of the tension between projected heterosexuality and the internally complex masculinity that was the basis for *Seinfeld*'s sexual humour. When Jerry buys himself an expensive suede jacket, he asks George's opinion. George tells Jerry that despite his 'resolute heterosexuality', Jerry's jacket is 'fabulous', a deliberately camp choice of words. Oddly, the jacket isn't all that great, although it does have a hot pink striped lining. Little wonder that later in the episode, Elaine's parodically masculine father – war veteran, Scotch drinker, consumer of insanely hot curries – thinks that George is gay.

Soon George himself is wondering if he is gay. In 'The Note' (episode 18, 1991), George has a massage from a rather good-looking man called Raymond. During the course of this treatment, George thinks that 'it moved'. That movement is 'the test' for homosexuality in his view. Although Jerry reassures him that this does not mean that he is gay, the grounds are a little tenuous. Jerry claims that the 'test is contact' – that the movement must result from direct physical contact. George continues to obsess over the issue and finds that men are popping into his sexual fantasies despite his best efforts to keep them out. In his closing monologue, Jerry speculates that the cause of homophobia is that men have 'weak sales resistance'. Men are easily sold shoes that they don't like or trousers that don't fit because it's easier than saying no. The theory goes that if you found yourself in a 'homosexual store', you might easily be talked into the sale. Without overlooking the obvious comic intent, this parallel between sexuality and shopping is notably anti-essentialist. Sexuality is here as much a matter of opportunity and approach as it is one of any fundamental predilection. So George's future fiancée, Susan Ross (Heidi Swedberg), discovers after a fire that her father had had a passionate affair with the writer John Cheever, whom he calls 'the love of my life', despite his apparently staid Upper-East-Side lifestyle. Cheever himself had been similarly closeted, but it was a surprisingly literary reference for a sitcom (episode 48, 'The Cheever Letters', 1992). Susan herself became a lesbian after her first dalliance with George, it might be remembered (episode 61, 'The Smelly Car', 1993). The target of *Seinfeld*'s humour in these instances is homophobia, not homosexuality. While that might seem unremarkable today, this was an unusual approach in 1991. It was only a year since Queer Nation had made their demonstration on the *Arsenio Hall Show*. In 1989, the rather pious drama *thirtysomething* had lost over

$1 million in advertising revenue because of a scene showing two gay men talking in bed. The point here is not to 'out' *Seinfeld* as a gay show, which it was not, but to think about the ways in which it included the possibility of same-sex attraction in masculine identity. In a culture that worries about the slightest deviation from an absurd caricature of he-man masculinity, that inclusion did make *Seinfeld* queer, if queer is a way of thinking about sexuality as a range of possibilities rather than as a binary opposition between radically different poles.

In its first incarnation as *The Seinfeld Chronicles*, the show had no 'Elaine' character or any starring women. In his stand-up and in the action of this pilot episode, Jerry dwells at length on his inability to understand women, so much so that he compares interpreting what women think to a murder investigation. This line of thought recurs when Jerry is explaining to the 'real' Elaine why there was no Elaine character in the show-within-the-show *Jerry*. The character of Elaine

Jerry and Elaine, who refused to live happily ever after

was added to the cast in the first series of *Seinfeld* at the insistence of TV executives, notionally to appeal to women but also to distance any suspicion that these single men might be in and out of each other's apartments for more than conversation. If *Seinfeld* shared with Freud the insight that all sexuality is bisexuality, it also shared his despairing inability to understand women. Freud was reduced to asking: 'What does a woman want?'. This bafflement is shared by the majority of American men whether gay, straight, transgendered or queer. It follows that Elaine in both her 'real' and 'fictional' versions within *Seinfeld* and *Jerry* was written essentially as a single man – sarcastic, physically assertive, cigar-smoking, willing to go to sports games and even prepared to make deals for casual sex. In 'The Deal' (episode 14, 1991), Jerry and Elaine decide to reopen their friendship to '*that*', circumscribed by certain rules such as 'spending the night is optional' and 'no calls the day after *that*'. Here is the ideal relationship for a certain sort of man: friendship, sex and no emotional commitment of any kind. Jerry blows the deal when he tries to sustain the lack of commitment by giving Elaine cash for her birthday, while Kramer presents her with a bench that she has been wanting. From this point on, Jerry and Elaine are – with one or two exceptions – not a couple and that was essential for the series to function in the way that it did.

Compared to the standard long-suffering but physically attractive girlfriend or wife in comedies of the time, Elaine was a very different character, albeit one generated by the accident that Larry David and Jerry Seinfeld themselves believed that they could not write convincing women characters. By default, they created a version for Elaine of what queer theorist Judith Halberstam has called 'female masculinity'.[31] Although the 'tough gal' sidekick was a known quantity, this form of gendering was not represented in a lead role in mass popular culture until Kimberley Pierce's biopic of Brandon Teena, *Boys Don't Cry* (2000). So Elaine's female masculinity remained in effect invisible on the show as a queer moment that was nonetheless perfectly there. By being positioned as Jerry's ex-girlfriend, Elaine was a different type of comic woman character, unlikely to have a romantic interface

'So you think you're sponge-worthy?'

Elaine on her way to be best man at a lesbian wedding

either with the lead or his friends. She was at first rather sharp, even unpleasant. In the first episode, she is only willing to go out if she doesn't have to talk ('Good News, Bad News', 1989). In the next one ('The Stakeout', 1990), she argues sharply with Jerry over his flirting with someone else and it is only at the end of the show that they agree that it is going to be necessary for them to discuss the other people they are dating. Elaine becomes more sympathetic as the show goes on, at least within the circle. But there is a certain animosity, which she explains to a fellow subway rider: 'I hate men. But I'm not a lesbian.' However, she is certainly known in lesbian circles, because she was on her way to be best man at a lesbian wedding, long before such events were the stuff of national debate (episode 30, 'The Subway', 1992). So here *Seinfeld* wants to suggest that the 'test' for lesbianism is not necessarily hating men. When Susan is dating women after leaving him, George theorises that he has driven her to it, acting out of the old joke that goes: MAN: 'Are you a lesbian?' WOMAN: 'Are you the

Susan about to be vomited on by Kramer

alternative?' George knows that if he is the alternative, lesbianism must
be very attractive. At the same time, he himself finds it equally attractive,
leading him to try and date Susan again. Sexual identity flows in ways
that are certainly comic by virtue of being ridiculous but also suggest an
openness to gender and sexual difference that was by no means typical
of American television of the period.

This openness should not be surprising. Gender flexibility had
been a key part of Jewish entertainment from the era before mass media,
while Yiddish theatre had long played with cross-dressing and gender
queering. Oscar Wilde was inspired by Yiddish theatre in the East End
of London in the early 1890s, where he might have seen the legendary
actor Jacob Adler. Wilde later sent his character Dorian Gray to a
similar theatre, where he falls in love with one of the actresses. Yiddish
plays themselves were sometimes a parody of Western theatre, as in *The
Yiddish Hamlet*, sometimes serious plays or operettas but most
frequently comedies and vaudeville shows. When he encountered it as a
young man in Prague, the novelist Franz Kafka found it fascinating. In
October 1911, Kafka visited the Café Savoy in Prague where he saw a
Yiddish theatre troupe starring Flora Klug, a drag king he called 'Mrs. K
"male impersonator" ', and her husband, who performed as a kind of
chorus. Kafka saw these actors as 'people who are Jews in an especially
pure form because they live only in the religion, but live in it without
effort, understanding, or distress'. Yet their theatrical mode was comedy:

> They seem to make a fool of everyone, laugh immediately after the
> murder of a noble Jew, sell themselves to an apostate, dance with their
> hands on their earlocks in delight when the unmasked murderer poisons
> himself and calls upon God, and yet all this because they are as light as a
> feather … are sensitive, cry easily with dry faces.[32]

Satirical, emotionally shallow and yet buffeted by the storms of everyday
life, these characters are prototypes for the *Seinfeld* team. These earlier
modes of Jewish performance would have been well known to the New
York Jewish comedians who made *Seinfeld*. The legendary Yiddish

theatre actress Molly Picon (1898–1992), for example, began her career with a 'trousers' role playing the lead in *Schmendrik* (1887), a play so popular that the word entered both Yiddish and New York slang to mean a lovable fool.[33] Her other male roles, such as Yonkele, set the precedent for Barbra Streisand's cross-dressed role as a Yeshiva student in *Yentl* (1983). After many appearances on stage and screen, Picon was immortalised in the role of the matchmaker Yente in the stage and film version of *Fiddler on the Roof* (1971). In the heart of the old Jewish theatre district on Second Avenue in the East Village, the Second Avenue Deli just around the corner from my office, had an entire room devoted to her career. I went there to mourn the Bush election victory of 2004, but as if to say that four more years were more than it could stand, the Deli closed soon afterwards.

Reversal of gender stereotypes was the subject of the first hour-long *Seinfeld*, in which Jerry becomes friends with the former Mets first baseman Keith Hernandez (episode 34, 'The Boyfriend', 1992). They meet in a gym locker room, an almost parodically gay meeting-place, and from then on their friendship develops according to the logic of dating. Jerry worries about whether the shirt he is wearing is right, asks everyone why they think Keith hasn't called and gets jealous when Keith makes a date with Elaine. Here the writing gets tied up in itself: if Jerry is playing the female role to Keith's male, what is Elaine's position? So she ends up saying repeatedly, 'Jerry, he's a guy', or variations to that effect. The triangle collapses when Keith tries to go too far with Jerry too soon by asking him to help with a move. In the hierarchy of unpleasant requests from friends that cannot be turned down, moving is almost the worst but not quite as bad as the drive to the airport – in New York this can be over an hour each way, if you're unlucky with traffic. When Jerry tells Kramer of Keith's request, he is outraged, exclaiming, 'But you hardly know the guy!'. Nonetheless, when Jerry turns Keith down in an emotional outburst – 'I'm sorry, I just can't!' – it's of course Kramer who steps into the gap. Just as Elaine indicates that Keith is not going to get past third base with her, so Jerry is unable to go all the way into a male relationship. Elaine's break-up with Keith lacks comic punch –

it's because he turns out to be a smoker – suggesting that there was still not quite the space for a woman in the ensemble.

So by the time episode 57 (11 February 1993) was called 'The Outing', it was clear that it was not a daytrip being depicted. A college reporter from NYU thinks she overhears Jerry and George debating whether to come out as a gay couple, but they know she is listening and are pretending. George has gone too far, of course, and declares to Jerry that 'You're the only man I ever loved', which, in the context of the show, might well be true. When the reporter later comes by Jerry's apartment to interview him, she recognises them from the coffee shop and interprets their banter over the cleanliness of a pear and the attractiveness of a shirt as couple-talk. When they talk about having met in a gym, she decides to out them. Her decision is met with a denial that is immediately disavowed: 'not that there's anything wrong with that!' This disavowal both makes what would otherwise seem like prejudice into a ridiculous exposure of the difficulty of claiming heterosexuality and undermines the force of that claim. Part of the internal pun here is that Jerry himself plays the comedic straight man in part in direct

107

'Not that there's anything wrong with that!'

imitation of Jack Benny, who had played the 'straight' man with a noticeably queer affect. Jerry's signature line in the mature *Seinfeld* is 'Now let me get this straight', when, for example, George is describing eating an eclair that he found in the garbage (episode 92, 'The Gymnast', 1994). In Jerry's closing stand-up, he claimed that because he was 'thin, single and neat', people assumed that he was gay, reflecting what has just 'happened'. Although his sneaker-wearing persona seems an unlikely model for urban queerness, there were many rumours to that effect at the time. In the stand-up, Jerry wonders what it must be like for gay men who are fat and messy, imagining that people say to them '"Y'know Joe, I enjoy being gay with you but I think it's about time, y'know, that you got in shape, tucked the shirt in and lost the wife" ' (episode 57, 'The Outing' 1993). In other words, Jerry's 'signals' read gay, although he himself was not. Again, this repeated denial seems to call attention to exactly that which it was trying to deny, creating comedy from the imprecise intersection between a weakly projected heterosexuality and a dubious identification with masculinity.

Attributing a zone of sexuality to a person who does not remain rigidly fixed at one of the presumed binary poles of 'straight' and 'gay' suited the sense of an era that turned 'gay vague' into a form of marketing. The term was coined by Michael Wilke in the journal *Advertising Age* in 1997, meaning ads that implied or suggested a gay affect but in such a way that it could be plausibly denied. The commercial most associated with this trend was called 'Sunday Afternoon' made to promote the Volkswagen Golf. It showed two men silently driving around inspecting furniture that people have thrown out – something of a sport on the days when this kind of garbage disposal is allowed in New York – and first recovering and then rejecting a chair. Shown to the soundtrack of the 1980s' Trio song 'Da, Da, Da', the ad was first shown during *Ellen*'s coming-out episode, seeming to confirm its queerness. However, straight men apparently assumed that the two were simply roommates.[34] In the early 1990s, commentators came up with the term 'metrosexual' to describe men who used moisturiser, worked out, matched their socks to their shirts, but tended to be straight. It resurfaced with a vengeance around 2000 when celebrities, as well as ordinary men, began performing metrosexuality. The football (soccer) player David Beckham was the archetype of this celebrity metrosexual, participating in a boy's dream career, married to a girl-band singer – Posh of the Spice Girls, aka Victoria Beckham – and willing to wear a skirt in public.

The unspoken question in much of the media commentary about metrosexuality was whether its actual sexual practice was different or distinct from heterosexuality. *Seinfeld*'s explorations of the topic suggest that metrosexuality was characterised more by failure than any radical transformation of sexual life. Like the 'gay vague' advertising of the period, *Seinfeld* alluded to its sex life rather than giving it names, let alone actually showing it. Unlike a previous generation of comedians from Lenny Bruce to Richard Pryor for whom naming the previously unnameable was the source of comic affect and a presumed social benefit, *Seinfeld* found ways to create comedy from sexual failure that did not name its object and by alluding to a desire that in prime time had not yet been able to say its name. One of the best-known episodes of the entire series never named its subject, to wit the legendary 'Contest' (episode 51, 1992). The premise of the episode was that George was alone in his parents' house, where he saw a copy of *Glamour* magazine. His mother, who came home early, was surprised to see him 'treating his body like it was an amusement park'. Recalling the event in the coffee shop, with the combination of extreme embarrassment and the injury caused to his mother when she fell over in shock, George resolves to abstain from the activity ever again. Meeting with widespread disbelief, George suggests a contest, with a cash prize for the person who holds out against temptation longest. At first the contest is with Jerry but Kramer jumps in despite Jerry's assertion that 'you'll be out before we get the check'. When Elaine also wants to compete, the men assert that she has to put up at least a double stake because 'men have to do it, it's part of our lifestyle'. Here Elaine makes it explicit that she wants to be one of the boys but she is immediately seen as having an advantage over them. Although Kramer is indeed out of the contest moments later, because he can see a woman walking around naked in the next apartment building –

109

shades of Hitchcock's 1954 classic *Rear Window* here – Elaine does not win. She is undone by meeting John F. Kennedy Jr in her aerobics class and the promise of a date with this member of American 'royalty' undermines her resolve. In the metrosexual world, celebrity is the ultimate aphrodisiac. While it is never clear who won the contest, the group clearly failed in its efforts at self-control.

The more conventional form of sexual failure, male and female, was evoked shortly afterwards (episode 65, 'The Mango,' 1993). In a coffee-shop discussion about women 'faking', Elaine pointedly names the object of the fake: 'Orgasm?'. George and Jerry are insistent that they would know. Unfortunately for Jerry, Elaine then points out that he had not known when she faked. Flabbergasted, he asks, 'but what about the breathing, the panting, the moaning, the screaming?', to which Elaine theatrically replies, 'Fake! Fake! Fake! Fake! Not bad, huh?' Viewers with a long memory might recall at this point that when Jerry explained to his parents why he and Elaine had broken up back in the first series, he did mention a 'problem with the physical chemistry'. His parents

The tense moment of condom unwrapping

assumed that the problem in question was that Jerry did not find Elaine
sufficiently attractive but this unlikely explanation now stands corrected.
Elaine's coffee-shop revelation recalls Meg Ryan's performance of a fake
orgasm in the Lower-East-Side Jewish delicatessen Katz's in the film
*When Harry Met Sally* (1989). Like the *Seinfeld* boys, Harry (Billy
Crystal) has asserted that he would of course know if a woman faked it,
so Sally sets out to prove him wrong. Elaine brings the question closer to
home by removing the sense that this is just a generic possibility and
recasting an entire relationship. The news disturbs both George and Jerry
to such an extent that they both experience the male inability to perform.
By their own lights, the hapless twosome have failed not only in a given
situation but also what one would have to call the 'test' for
heterosexuality. If the 'test' is response to contact, then both men have
struck out and must be accounted non-heterosexuals.

Still nothing
wrong with that

111

Perhaps this conceit that there is no proper way to 'test' for sexuality except in action accounts for the extraordinary demand for drugs like Viagra to counter impotence. Viagra prescriptions averaged 300,000 a week in 2003, with global sales amounting to approximately US $2.5bn. What Viagra's effects prove to their subject is not simply a renewed potency but a confirmed membership of the sexually active club. Yet it seems that, like Groucho Marx, some men are finding that any club that wants them is one they do not want to belong to, as Viagra sales declined by 10 per cent in 2004. The *New York Times* lined up a Harvard urologist Dr Abraham Morgentaler to declare: 'I don't think there's anything wrong with that.'[35] We already know that there's nothing wrong with being gay. Now, to much greater relief for all men, everyone's impotent and there's nothing wrong with that. One of the most notable televisual uses of Viagra recently appeared on the HBO series *Big Love*, which tells the story of a Mormon family in Utah where one man has three improbably beautiful wives. Nonetheless, with all the bed-hopping, Bill Henrikson (played by Bill Paxton) soon finds himself popping Viagras to keep up with his wives' competition to be Number One in his physical, and hence financial, affections (episode 2, 'Viagra Blue', 2005). While HBO might have hoped for a little ratings-boosting scandal, the series did not arouse much concern, as it was so clearly *Desperate Housewives* (2004–) with the twist that they're all married to the same man.

At the same time, *Big Love*'s veneer of religiosity does speak to a tension in American life between its Christian and Puritan 'founders' and both the original inhabitants of the continent and subsequent non-Christian or secular immigrants. If the American earthly paradise is by definition Christian, how do non-Christians become American? The Canadian-born Jew of Russian descent Saul Bellow declared in his famous opening to *The Adventures of Augie March* (1953) that 'I am an American, Chicago born.' When post-war Jewish artists and intellectuals read that line, they had to decide what it meant for them. For one set of secular Jews in the 1960s and 1970s, the answer was to pursue a paradisical sexuality. The character Nathan Zuckerman in

Philip Roth's novels engaged in all manner of sexual adventures, one of which involving liver, in *Portnoy's Complaint* (1969), left George in the shade for solitary activity in the parental home. Woody Allen made this unbound Jewish libido the centre of his now much-lamented early films. The Long Island-born comedian Lenny Bruce was arrested for obscenity in 1961 for discussing the etymology of 'to come' in a way that would no longer raise either an eyebrow or a laugh. The emergence of a comedy of sexual failure and inadequacy in *Seinfeld* was in part a reaction against this earlier generation's need to reiterate the heroic sexuality of American Jews. In moving away from a sense of Jewishness as defined by tragedy, *Seinfeld* was able to find its obsession with sex as ridiculous as it was.

This dynamic was central to an episode that balanced the myth of the female gymnast and the male comedian as exemplary performers (episode 92, 'The Gymnast', 1994). Jerry meets Katya, a Romanian woman who had won a silver medal for gymnastics at the 1984 Olympics (Romania was the only Soviet-bloc country to compete at the 1984 Los Angeles Olympics and two women won silvers for gymnastics, Ekaterina Szabó and Doina Staiculescu). He does not feel inclined to pursue the relationship but Kramer insists that he is on the verge of 'sensual delights most men can only dream of'. To clinch his case, Kramer shows Jerry a tape of Katya performing and thereby instils in him the fantasy that he might become the 'apparatus' in an encounter. Although the tryst takes place, results are ordinary, leaving Jerry with the obligation to put in a few weeks of pretend-relationship before ending the affair. However, Katya ends the affair herself, saying that

> In my country, they speak of a man so virile, so potent, that to spend a night with such a man is to enter a world of such sensual delights most women dare not dream of. This man is known as the 'Comedian'. You may tell jokes, Mr Jerry Seinfeld, but you are no 'Comedian'.

Neither performer finds the other the stuff of which dreams are made and in the end it seems that the fantasy of sensual excess is simply that:

a fantasy. If, as the philosopher Judith Butler has convinced a generation of young people, gender and sexuality are things that you *do* rather than things that you *are* by definition, then it is also possible to do them badly.[36] For many, perhaps most people it may only be possible to do them badly and then laugh at the inevitable failures that result.

People fail to perform in a variety of interesting and unusual ways throughout the series. Elaine has a jazz-musician boyfriend in one episode who is very much to her taste even though he doesn't 'do everything' (episode 121, 'The Rye', 1996). The episode mirrors Jerry's earlier efforts to move up from the club scene, as John has a network scout coming to see his set. However, because John has heard that Elaine thinks they are 'hot and heavy', he decides to add to his repertoire in the bedroom. Unfortunately, as an apparent novice in the art, his efforts delay his arrival for the showcase until the last minute. When he gets up to play saxophone, his mouth has become so tired and dried out that he cannot produce a sound. In another discussion on the subject, George and Jerry have worried about what to do 'below the equator' and decide

114

'He doesn't do *everything*'

that no one knows, it's all a question of luck (episode 65, 'The Mango', 1993). If it seems that it is mostly men failing – and it is – it is not entirely one-way traffic. Elaine is asked by a gay friend to be his 'beard' for his employers, meaning a woman whose presence allows for a presumption of heterosexuality (episode 102, 'The Beard', 1995). Unfortunately, she has such a good time that she falls for him and tries to convert him back to what she and Jerry call 'our team'. For one exciting night she succeeds, giving hope to every woman who has had to say 'too bad he's gay', and opening a vista of endless sex and shopping. But alas, he returns to his own team because, as the home team, they have so much more experience with the equipment. Which is why, as Jerry puts it, 'they lose very few players'. The *Seinfeld* characters were really only confident when playing with their own equipment by themselves.

So it was scarcely surprising that the closest Jerry came to making a commitment on the show was when he met a woman almost exactly like him (episode 134, 'The Invitations', 1996). Jeannie Steinman (Janeane Garofalo) eats cereal in restaurants, asks what the

115

Jerry discovers he is his own ideal

deal is with everything and even has the same initials as Jerry. He feels a tide of emotion and suddenly comes to a realisation of 'what it is I've been looking for all these years. Myself! And now I've swept myself off my feet!'. An engagement is announced, but before long 'wiser' counsels are prevailing, when Kramer advises Jerry that marriage is a 'man-made prison' (as if there was another kind of prison: so does he mean literally made by men to imprison themselves?). Even more problematic for Jerry is that he realises that he can't be with someone like him – 'I hate myself!' The intense narcissistic identification that made the idea of the relationship work is inevitably subverted by a paranoia that anyone like him could not be any good. So prone are the characters to failure that they can even fail at breaking up. While he is being 'outed' as Jerry's partner, George was stuck in a relationship with a woman named Alison even though he had tried to break up with her, then claimed to be gay and finally 'outed' himself as the porn actor Buck Naked – all to no avail (episode 57, 'The Outing', 1993). So it was no surprise that once he had

116

Susan dies by toxic envelope

become engaged to Susan, against all logic and reason, George is unable to make the engagement fail and equally unable just to call it off, because he could not face the scene that would ensue. In the case of a real person, one might speculate that he in fact wanted to be married more than he could admit to his friends and even to himself, but such depth of character was not part of being George Costanza. In different episodes, he tries smoking, asking for a prenuptial agreement and other devices, only to fall short. It is only when another man, whom George has similarly insulted, says to Susan that she could have done a lot better that she is prompted to consider her options. Nonetheless, she stays with George, until her untimely demise caused by toxic glue on the cheapest possible wedding invitations (episode 134, 'The Invitations', 1996).

At the same time, there was a certain misogyny at work in *Seinfeld*. George's reason for trying to break his engagement is that being married will kill off the side of his personality called 'coffee-shop George'. As this person is less than a resounding success in the world at large, it might be thought no particular cause for concern that he be laid to rest. But Kramer similarly convinces Jerry that marriage (or a live-in relationship) is to be avoided when he points out that in the evening you 'have to talk about your day. How was your day?' On more than one occasion, a woman challenges Jerry to kiss her and the viewer sees a full-screen shot of her puckered mouth that is presumably intended to be revolting. Certainly, Jerry declines the invitations to kiss both Margaret, who turns out to be Newman's ex (episode 88, 'The Big Salad', 1994), and later Jenna (Kristin Davis), who has used a toothbrush that fell into the toilet (episode 150, 'The Pothole', 1997) . But the emotion here is not so much hate as fear. Women seem to know things that the immature 'men' in *Seinfeld* do not. These men are excited at the chance to see a naked woman across the street, to see women fighting, aka a catfight, or to watch another naked woman brush her hair. An entire episode centred around the Miss America pageant, that adolescent version of the burlesque show (episode 97, 'The Chaperone', 1994). All of these mildly erotic moments are about watching rather than doing, reflecting a sexu-

117

ality that does not know what it is or what to do with itself and is therefore perfectly suited to television. It is this adolescent curiosity that
fuelled *Seinfeld*'s fascination with the everyday quirks in the social order,
those places where one does not quite know what the rules are, which are
pursued in the hope of a glimpse of the forbidden or exotic adult world.
These adult adolescents continue to be fascinated with Superman, can
cook nothing more sophisticated than cereal and cannot imagine how
other genders and sexualities think. What they can do is talk about it.

     This stasis ultimately had an effect on the characters as
characters. While it can be argued that George's unmitigated feelings of
relief when his fiancée Susan died were precisely in character, the
collective shrug with which the others received the news was clearly
heartless. Although Jerry and Elaine attended his distant cousin's
funeral after he killed her with the pony remark in the second series,
Susan's funeral is unremarked upon and unseen. When Kramer was
urging Jerry to pursue Katya the Romanian gymnast, Jerry replies that

118

Jerry unlikely date no. 200 or so: Courtney Cox

'unlike you I am in the unfortunate position of having to consider people's feelings'. This position became less credible as the procession of Jerry's ex-girlfriends swelled in number. At one point, he finds himself uncertain when he pays the maid, whom he is also dating, exactly which service he is paying for (episode 175, 'The Maid', 1998). Towards the end of the series, Jerry's character has changed, so that in one episode his girlfriend Patty tries to provoke some emotional response but he claims to simply be empty inside (episode 159, 'The Serenity Now', 1997). She teaches him how to get angry, which he begins to do on a regular basis. When Patty breaks up with him because of his new bad mood, he unaccountably gets upset, although, as Elaine puts it, he breaks up with a girl every week, which is to say, every episode. Suddenly, new emotional Jerry appears with the downside that 'I'm not funny any more'. The new caring Jerry proposes marriage to Elaine and invites George to come out of his shell as well. Listening to the full horrors of George's internal emotions snaps Jerry out of it and back into being funny, implying that *Seinfeld* understood humour as being incompatible with 'normal' heterosexual adult relationships. Its choice was for the 'queer time' of eternal conversation, coffee and the dialectics of dating, as opposed to the 'family time' of school schedules, play dates and regular work.[37] In this sense, *Seinfeld* was never more than 'queer vague', as it were, in that queer time circles around clubs, bars and other scene places, whereas the *Seinfeld* characters eke out their days in a coffee shop, a one-bedroom apartment and at the gym.

119

These endless worries about dating seem decidedly passé these days. Rather than having to 'put in' relationship time after a sexual encounter, contemporary discussion about sex revolves around the friendship-free 'hook-up' or the relationship-free category of 'friends with benefits'. If George wanted to break up with Susan, all he would have to do is change his MySpace or Facebook page category to 'single' or 'it's complicated' from 'in a relationship'. What seems different is the very precision and explictness of the contemporary scene, in which things like pornography or lap-dancing get discussed on mainstream television as a matter of course. By contrast, *Seinfeld*'s most notorious (solo) sex act was provoked by a copy of *Glamour* magazine and no one visits any form of commercial sex establishment in all nine series – even *Friends* went to a strip club, booked a hooker instead of a stripper for a bachelor party and was latterly obsessed with online porn. One shudders to think of George watching *The L Word* or *Sex and the City*. At the same time, if Jerry found himself dating a person with 'man-hands', he might now have to suspect that his date was transgender or transvestite, rather than just not his perfect physical type. In the cable-dominated television world that has developed after the *Seinfeld* era, explicitness is a prerequisite for success.

The rapid air of anachronism attached to *Seinfeld* may account for what has become known as 'The Seinfeld Curse' that renders all the subsequent comedy ventures of the cast null and void. This condition affects the former cast members more than its principal. Having killed off 'Jerry Seinfeld' by sending him to prison, Seinfeld himself did one last tour of his material and retired it. He is now in semi-retirement, awaiting rediscovery by a generation that were children when *Seinfeld* was on in the background. For the other cast members, the curse has been more potent. Jason Alexander, Julia Louis-Dreyfus and Michael Richards have all had their own shows and all have been dreadful, not even 'so bad they're good', lasting hardly a season. Louis-Dreyfus has finally experienced a minor hit with her *Old Adventures of New Christine* (2006– ) but it is just the kind of suburban family 'comedy' that *Seinfeld* rightly detested. When Louis-Dreyfus did a promotional appearance for the series on *Saturday Night Live*, her *Seinfeld* cast members were good enough sports to do a segment or two about the *Seinfeld* curse, with Jerry manically cutting a light fixture to try and kill her and Alexander appearing as George, desperate for a job. He has little choice. When he appeared on Bill Maher's late-night satire and debate show on HBO in 2005, an army general who disagreed with Alexander's position on Iraq turned to him and said, 'Now, look here, George ...', at which point the audience broke up and the issue was forgotten. The other side of this dilemma was seen when Michael Richards attacked his hecklers in a comedy club. Their final retort as they were leaving was to point out that he had achieved nothing other than his role on *Seinfeld*. It was this remark that punctured his racist balloon, leading him to declare apparently sarcastically but also with some acceptance, 'Yeah, I'm all washed up.' After a moment's reflection, he dropped the mike and ran off the stage. When Richards appeared on TV to apologise, many remarked that his contrition might have been caused by the simultaneous release of season seven of *Seinfeld* on DVD. *Seinfeld*'s cast are prisoners of their past performances, unable to escape their function as a remembrance of past time for other people. It's a gilded cage to be sure, but an unexpected fate for the show about nothing.

# 6 New York, New York

At the time Jerry Seinfeld and Larry David were trying to make it as comedians in the late 1970s, New York grit was more than ordinarily required. The city was on the verge of bankruptcy in 1977, but the Federal Government of then-President Gerald Ford refused to assist it, prompting the legendary headline: 'Ford to City: Drop Dead'. With street-crime levels high, exacerbated by drug-gang warfare, the beginning of the AIDS epidemic and financial crisis created a sense of terminal decline. New Yorkers often revel in this practical difficulty, advising those who find it too hard to move to Westchester, the epitome of the comfortable but boring suburbs. The television series *Seinfeld* was one sign of the city's eventual recovery in the 1990s. By a curious and final irony, the show is itself now a digital avatar for a past time, circulating in the half-life of reruns and on DVD. At a certain point the reruns were beginning to diminish in frequency and it looked as if *Seinfeld* would become a late-night obscurity, soon to become extinct. Once the first shock of 9/11 had worn off and the dire prophecies about the return to moral seriousness and the end of irony had themselves come to seem silly, a reversal happened. In 2006, a viewer in New York can easily see three episodes of *Seinfeld* a day, and on some days six, broadcast at popular times. All these repeats are shown on network or basic cable stations reaching the largest fraction of the remaining TV audience.

None of *Seinfeld*'s jokes can be new to anyone who is not a recent immigrant and the situations they refer to are a thing of the past.

No young person could afford a market-rate rental apartment on the Upper-West side these days, especially if living by themselves. Today aspiring young professionals head to Brooklyn and even Queens, and tend to look down on Manhattan as passé and old. But in writing this book, I have never been able to mention the project without my listener interrupting with their favourite sequence or episode. *Seinfeld* has entered the urban mythology of New York as an entrance requirement. It embodies and makes visible the New York insistence that the city was better 'before' the present and has declined into its current condition. At the same time, there is a political nostalgia for the Clinton era that has even made Al Gore a popular repeat performer on *Saturday Night Live*. The very verbal acuity of *Seinfeld* contrasts with the inarticulate and incoherent violence of the Bush era, epitomised by his smirk and Cheney's manifest evil.

In a time when Secretary of Defense Donald Rumsfeld dismissed the looting of Baghdad in 2003 with the phrase 'stuff happens', comedy has taken two divergent paths. On the one hand, there is a newly angry comedy, as if reverting to the Lenny Bruce era, that is represented by *Curb Your Enthusiasm*. Larry David is reworking many of the themes he began in *Seinfeld* but in a more embarrassing and angry style. Where George was a wannabe bra salesman, the 'Larry David' character in *Curb* asks his Latina maid what bra size she uses. While George ranted about Ted Danson getting paid better than he was, 'Larry David' yells directly at Ted Danson about his choice of chef for their restaurant. While the series remains outside of formal politics, its manifest rage at the world and its espousal of environmental issues makes it in some sense oppositional. Rage is not in itself a progressive emotion and there is more than enough to go around, as a cursory glance at the right-wing blogs collectively known as the 'wingnutosphere' will amply prove. On television, the cable news channels convey more rage in an evening than any comedy series could deliver. Perhaps comedic rage was only effective as satire when the affect of the mainstream was steadily calm and patrician. The deadpan news parodies of Jon Stewart and Stephen Colbert on Comedy Central's

123

*The Daily Show* and *The Colbert Report* have had more bite in their consistent attempt to expose the logic of the current administration for what it is in its own terms. So when Vice-President Dick Cheney shot his hunting partner in 2006, Stewart's tactic was 'to take a moment', in which he silently drank tea and savoured the full richness of the irony that a man so widely associated with war and torture that he had been dubbed the 'Vice-President for Torture' had perpetrated this of all accidents. For the rest of the week, *The Daily Show* had its fake correspondents loudly utter the simple truth: 'Vice-President Dick Cheney has shot a seventy-eight-year-old man [pause] *in the face*!'. The laugh came from the Pinter-esque pause played for laughs, with the emphasis creating a ridiculous representation of the Vice-President as living up to his own stereotype.

By way of alternative, the Bush years have also seen the emergence into the mainstream of a form of comedy that is sympathetic to the prevalent political winds. *Blue Collar Comedy* uses a revue format in which a series of mostly white male comedians from the South perform observational comedy from their regional and cultural perspective, reinforced by appropriate musical guests and viewer contests. *Blue Collar Comedy* has had significant success first as a live event, then as direct-to-DVD films, followed by cinematic releases and finally a TV series called *Blue Collar TV* (2004–5). Blue collar is opposed to white collar as the work clothes of a manual or industrial worker rather than an office or managerial worker. The *Blue Collar* franchise thus addresses one of the Republican Party's core constituencies, the white working classes of the South and those who identify with that perspective from other socioeconomic groups. In a typically American paradox, blue-collar people consider themselves middle class because they are actively employed, as opposed to being on welfare, being lazy or doing a non-job, like office work. The show is headlined by Jeff Foxworthy whose not very successful sitcom *The Jeff Foxworthy Show* (1995) was screened on ABC during the *Seinfeld* years. The jokes run along the lines of (to take the example of Foxworthy's album title): 'You're a redneck if … your tires cost more than the truck'. On the TV show, he had a segment in which people sent in photos to contest for 'Redneck Yard of the Week', scoring points for cars without wheels propped up on bricks, disconnected washing machines and other telling details. The jokes are often centred around the failures of marriage, such as men forgetting anniversaries, that have long been the staple of television comedy. But in between these standard remarks comes a consistent series of jibes against affirmative action, Rosie O'Donnell (an actress and talk-show host who has attracted criticism since coming out as a lesbian) and any sign of effeminacy, let alone homosexuality, in men. I was struck by a moment in which one comedian won a passionate round of screaming applause just for the line 'I'm an American.' This affirmation is taken to be in opposition to what the talk-radio crowd call the 'Hate America First' East-Coast liberals, also known as the Jews. By contrast, the performers like to make a slip where they say 'Black, I'm sorry, I mean African-American' that also brings the house down. Here the fake disavowal of prejudice is the target of the joke, as the audience at once recognises.

*Blue Collar TV* was not wildly successful but it has established a solid niche for itself, compelling a mainstream counterpart in NBC's successful series *My Name is Earl* (2005–) that also centres around a self-described redneck. Earl is prompted to reconsider his life after he loses a winning lottery ticket when he is hit by a passing truck. Recovering in hospital, he sees Carson Daly of *Queer Eye for the Straight Guy* (2003–6) talking about karma and is converted to the idea, insofar as he decides to make amends for all the things he has done wrong in the past. *Earl* has its funny moments and it's certainly not *Frasier*. But it's miles from *Blue Collar*'s world: no one there would know what karma was, and if they did they wouldn't like it, especially if it was introduced by a self-described queer. One side of America seems unfathomably strange to the other at the moment. A hit book recently asked *What's Wrong with Kansas?* (2004), meaning why do blue-collar people in Kansas vote Republican? *Blue Collar TV* knows the answer to that, except it's the wrong question: for them, the question is what's wrong with you, meaning 'the liberal elite'?

125

This divide meets in New York, which has become two cities since the terrorist attacks of 11 September 2001. Now the Frank Sinatra song 'New York, New York' is a description not a repetition. One is the destination of a certain form of atrocity tourism, centred on the site of the World Trade Center towers, now known portentously as Ground Zero. From there, the visitor from 'Kansas' or other traditionally anti-New York locations might go to a fire station to see the heroes of the day or to a Disney musical in the newly cleaned-up Times Square. Manhattan residents who vote 80 per cent Democrat, veering towards 90 per cent downtown and on the Upper West Side, are bemused by all this and try to avoid it, still seeking the New York of the mind that is rather thin on the ground these days. Oddly, *Seinfeld* can be the show for both New Yorks, representing either the last days before Bush, or the last days before the war on terror. As a creature of its time, *Seinfeld* was always carefully triangulated between the political poles, as mandated by Bill Clinton's success. In 'The Non-Fat Yogurt' (episode 71, 1993), in which supposedly non-fat yogurt was in fact loaded with it, the action took place during the mayoral election between David Dinkins and Rudolph Guiliani. Endings were filmed with both candidates but because the Republican Guiliani won, he appeared on the show. Fittingly, perhaps, Guiliani became known for his penchant for appearing in drag at various events before his actions during the attack on the World Trade Center earned him an honorary cowboy status. This time, which has become known as the era of terrorism, is clearly no longer 'about nothing'. If *Seinfeld* expressed its own era with some precision as a self-absorbed fascination with language and its ramifications, it can now be viewed as a nostalgic window into the past and perhaps as a hope for a better future. It has become a TV classic.

126

# Resources

(current in March 2007)

For scripts, episode guide and fan fiction, see <www.seinology.com>.

For episode list, guide and cast details, see
<www.tv.com/seinfeld/show/112/summary.html?tag=tabs;summary>.

For episode list with air times, see <epguides.com/Seinfeld>.

# Notes

**1** Roland Barthes, *Camera Lucida: Reflections on Photography* (New York: Noonday, 1981), p. 10.

**2** Ellen Fein and Sherrie Shamoon, *The Rules* (New York: Warner, 1995), p. 2.

**3** Raymond Williams, *Television: Technology and Cultural Form* (Hanover, NH and London: Wesleyan University Press [1974], rpr. 1992), pp. 85–7.

**4** There is a reference to the nineteenth-century American novelist Henry James (episode 173, 'The Bookstore', 1998) and an early episode circulates around Henry Miller's *Tropic of Cancer* (episode 22, 'The Library', 1991).

**5** Quoted by Geoffrey O'Brien, 'Sein of the Times', *New York Review of Books* vol. 44 no. 13 (14 August 1997).

**6** Jon Stratton's essay on *Seinfeld* similarly argues for the importance of 'civility' to the show in his *Coming Out Jewish: Constructing Ambivalent Identities* (New York and London: Routledge, 2000), pp. 282–314.

**7** Benjamin Spock and Michael B. Rothernberg, *Dr Spock's Baby and Child Care* (New York and London: Pocket Books, 1992), p. 458.

**8** Norbert Elias, *The Civilizing Process* (New York and Oxford: Blackwell, 2000).

**9** Jedediah Purdy, *For Common Things: Irony, Trust and Commitment in America Today* (New York: Knopf, 1999).

**10** Citations from Purdy, *For Common Things*, pp. i–24.

**11** Barthes, *Camera Lucida*, p. 30.

**12** Aristotle, 'Poetics', in *The Complete Works of Aristotle*, vol. 2, edited by Jonathan Barnes (Princeton, NJ: Princeton University Press, 1984), p. 2320.

**13** Ibid., p. 2319.

**14** Umberto Eco, *The Name of the Rose* (New York: Harcourt Brace, 1983), p. 468.

**15** Ibid., p. 475.

**16** Alexander Doty, *Making Things Perfectly Queer: Interpreting Mass Culture* (Minneapolis: University of Minnesota Press, 1993), p. 67.

**17** Kathleen Tracy, *Jerry Seinfeld: The Entire Domain* (Secaucus, NJ: Birch Lane Press, 1998), p. 85.

**18** Richard J. Hernnstein and Charles Murray, *The Bell Curve: Intelligence and Class Structure in American Life* (New York: Free Press, 1994).

**19** Similar accusations can be found on a fanatical website (even if now out of date) at <www.heretical.com/British/mindbend/broad.html>.

**20** See Susan Murray, 'Ethnic Masculinity and Early Television's Vaudeo Star', *Cinema Journal* vol. 42 no. 1 (Autumn 2002), pp. 97–119.

**21** Quoted by Stratton, *Coming Out Jewish*, p. 291.

**22** Jerry Oppenheimer, *Seinfeld: The Making of an American Icon. The Unauthorized Biography* (New York: HarperCollins, 2002), p. 238.

**23** Quoted by Doty, *Making Things Perfectly Queer*, p. 66. Doty does not mention the misogyny in the comment.

**24** Quoted by Rachel Adams, *Side Show U.S.A.: Freaks and the American Cultural Imagination* (Chicago, IL: Chicago University Press, 2001), p. 37.

**25** For an alternative view, see Carla Johnson, 'The Schlemiel and the Schlimazl in *Seinfeld*', *Journal of Popular Film and Television* vol. 22 no. 3 (1994), pp. 116–23.

**26** Bill Clinton, *My Life* (New York: Knopf, 2004), p. 543.

**27** Neal Gabler, *An Empire of Their Own: How the Jews Invented Hollywood* (New York: Bantam, 1989).

**28** Zygmund Bauman, *Modernity and the Holocaust* (Ithaca, NY: Cornell University Press, 1989). See also Primo Levi, *If Not Now When* (New York: Touchstone, 1995), also known as *Survival in Auschwitz*.

**29** Frantz Fanon, *Black Skin, White Masks* (New York: Grove, 1967).

**30** Susan Sontag, 'Notes on Camp' [1964], rpr. in *Against Interpretation* (New York: Picador [1966], 2001), n. 57.

**31** Judith Halberstam, *Female Masculinity* (Durham, NC and London: Duke University Press, 1998).

**32** Franz Kafka, *Diaries 1910–23*, edited by Max Brod (New York: Schocken, 1974), pp. 64–5.

**33** For details, see Jewish Women's Archive, 'JWA Molly Picon Introduction', at <www.jwa.org/exhibits/wov/picon/index.html> (6 September 2006).

**34** See <www.commercialcloset.org/cgi-bin/iowa/portrayals.html?record=43>, accessed 9 September 2006, for details, storyboard and a clip.

**35** Alex Berenson, 'Sales of Impotence Drugs Fall, Defying Expectations', *New York Times*, 4 December 2005.

**36** Judith Butler, *Gender Trouble* (London and New York: Routledge, 1990).

**37** Judith Halberstam, *In a Queer Time and Place* (New York: New York University Press, 2004).

# Credits

**Seinfeld**

**created by**
Larry David and Jerry Seinfeld

**executive producers**
Larry David
George Shapiro
Howard West
Fred Barron
Andrew Scheinman
Jerry Seinfeld

© Castle Rock Entertainment

**production companies**
*pilot*
Giggling Goose Productions,
Inc., in association with
Howard West and George
Shapiro Productions and
Castle Rock Entertainment

*series one*
A West/Shapiro production in
association with Fred Barron
Productions, Castle Rock
Entertainment

*series two to nine*
A West/Shapiro production in
association with Castle Rock
Entertainment

*main cast*
**Jerry Seinfeld**
himself
**Jason Alexander**
George Louis Costanza
**Michael Richards**
Cosmo Kramer
**Julia Louis-Dreyfus**
Elaine Marie Benes

*semi-regular cast*
**Wayne Knight**
Newman
**Larry David**
George Steinbrenner

**Estelle Harris**
Estelle Costanza
**Heidi Swedberg**
Susan Biddle Ross
**Jerry Stiller**
Frank Costanza
**Liz Sheridan**
Helen Seinfeld
**John O'Hurley**
J. Peterman
**Barney Martin**
Morty Seinfeld
**Len Lesser**
Uncle Leo

**broadcast history**
Transmitted in the US on
NBC (National Broadcasting
Corporation) from 5 July 1989
to 14 May 1998.
Nine seasons, a total of
180 x 22-minute episodes.

**pilot**
05/07/1990 The Seinfeld
                    Chronicles

**season one**
31/05/1990 The Stakeout
07/06/1990 The Robbery
14/06/1990 Male Unbonding
21/06/1990 The Stock Tip

**season two**
23/01/1991 The Ex-Girlfriend
30/01/1991 The Pony Remark
06/02/1991 The Jacket
13/02/1991 The Phone
                    Message
04/04/1991 The Apartment
11/04/1991 The Statue
18/04/1991 The Revenge
25/04/1991 The Heart Attack
02/05/1991 The Deal
16/05/1991 The Baby Shower
23/05/1991 The Chinese
                    Restaurant
26/06/1991 The Busboy

**season three**
18/09/1991 The Note
25/09/1991 The Truth
02/10/1991 The Pen
09/10/1991 The Dog
16/10/1991 The Library
30/10/1991 The Parking
                    Garage
06/11/1991 The Café
13/11/1991 The Tape
20/11/1991 The Nose Job
27/11/1991 The Stranded
04/12/1991 The Alternate
                    Side
11/12/1991 The Red Dot
08/01/1992 The Subway
15/01/1992 The Pez
                    Dispenser
29/01/1992 The Suicide
05/02/1992 The Fix-Up
12/02/1992 The Boyfriend
                    (part 1)
12/02/1992 The Boyfriend
                    (part 2)
26/02/1992 The Limo
04/03/1992 The Good
                    Samaritan
25/03/1992 The Letter
04/02/1992 The Parking Space
06/05/1992 The Keys

**season four**
12/08/1992 The Trip
                    (part 1)
19/08/1992 The Trip
                    (part 2)
09/09/1992 The Pitch
16/09/1992 The Ticket
23/09/1992 The Wallet
30/09/1992 The Watch
07/10/1992 The Bubble Boy
28/10/1992 The Cheever
                    Letters
04/11/1992 The Opera
11/11/1992 The Virgin
18/11/1992 The Contest
25/11/1992 The Airport
16/12/1992 The Pick
06/01/1993 The Movie

27/01/1993 The Visa
04/02/1993 The Shoes
11/02/1993 The Outing
18/02/1993 The Old Man
25/02/1993 The Implant
18/03/1993 The Junior Mint
15/04/1993 The Smelly Car
13/05/1993 The Handicap
    Spot
20/05/1993 The Pilot
    (part 1)
20/05/1993 The Pilot
    (part 2)

**season five**
16/09/1993 The Mango
23/09/1993 The Puffy Shirt
30/09/1993 The Glasses
07/10/1993 The Sniffiing
    Accountant
14/10/1993 The Bris
28/10/1993 The Lip Reader
04/11/1993 The Non-Fat
    Yogurt
11/11/1993 The Barber
18/11/1993 The Masseuse
09/12/1993 The Cigar Store
    Indian
16/12/1993 The Conversion
06/01/1994 The Stall
03/02/1994 The Dinner Party
10/02/1994 The Marine
    Biologist
17/02/1994 The Pie
24/02/1994 The Stand-In
17/03/1994 The Wife
28/04/1994 The Raincoats
    (part 1)
28/04/1994 The Raincoats
    (part 2)
05/05/1994 The Fire
12/05/1994 The Hamptons
19/05/1994 The Opposite

**season six**
22/09/1994 The Chaperone
29/09/1994 The Big Salad
06/10/1994 The Pledge Drive
13/10/1994 The Chinese
    Woman
27/10/1994 The Couch
03/11/1994 The Gymnast
10/11/1994 The Soup
17/11/1994 The Mom and Pop
    Store

08/12/1994 The Secretary
15/12/1994 The Race
05/01/1995 The Switch
19/01/1995 The Label Maker
26/01/1995 The Scoffllaw
02/02/1995 Highlights of a
    Hundred (part 1)
02/02/1995 Highlights of a
    Hundred (part 2)
09/02/1995 The Beard
16/02/1995 The Kiss Hello
23/02/1995 The Doorman
16/03/1995 The Jimmy
06/04/1995 The Doodle
27/04/1995 The Fusilli Jerry
04/05/1995 The Diplomat's
    Club
11/05/1995 The Face Painter
18/05/1995 The Understudy

**season seven**
21/09/1995 The Engagement
28/09/1995 The Postponement
05/10/1995 The Maestro
12/10/1995 The Wink
19/10/1995 The Hot Tub
02/11/1995 The Soup Nazi
09/11/1995 The Secret Code
16/11/1995 The Pool Guy
07/12/1995 The Sponge
14/12/1995 The Gum
04/01/1996 The Rye
25/01/1996 The Caddy
01/02/1996 The Seven
08/02/1996 The Cadillac
    (part 1)
08/02/1996 The Cadillac
    (part 2)
15/02/1996 The Shower Head
22/02/1996 The Doll
07/03/1996 The Friars Club
04/04/1996 The Wig Master
25/04/1996 The Calzone
02/05/1996 The Bottle
    Deposit (part 1)
02/05/1996 The Bottle
    Deposit (part 2)
09/05/1996 The Wait Out
16/05/1996 The Invitations

**season eight**
19/09/1996 The Foundation
26/09/1996 The Soul Mate
03/10/1996 The Bizarro Jerry
10/10/1996 The Little Kicks

17/10/1996 The Package
31/10/1996 The Fatigues
07/11/1996 The Checks
14/11/1996 The Chicken
    Roaster
21/11/1996 The Abstinence
19/12/1996 The Andrea Doria
09/01/1997 The Little Jerry
16/01/1997 The Money
30/01/1997 The Comeback
06/02/1997 The Van Buren
    Boys
13/02/1997 The Susie
20/02/1997 The Pothole
13/03/1997 The English
    Patient
10/04/1997 The Nap
24/04/1997 The Yada Yada
01/05/1997 The Millennium
08/05/1997 The Muffiin Tops
15/05/1997 The Summer of
    George

**season nine**
25/09/1997 The Butter Shave
02/10/1997 The Voice
09/10/1997 The Serenity Now
16/10/1997 The Blood
30/10/1997 The Junk Mail
06/11/1997 The Merv Griffin
    Show
13/11/1997 The Slicer
20/11/1997 The Betrayal
11/12/1997 The Apology
18/12/1997 The Strike
08/01/1998 The Dealership
15/01/1998 The Reverse
    Peephole
29/01/1998 The Cartoon
05/02/1998 The Strongbox
26/02/1998 The Wizard
19/03/1998 The Burning
09/04/1998 The Bookstore
23/04/1998 The Frogger
30/04/1998 The Maid
07/05/1998 The Puerto Rican
    Day
14/05/1998 The Clip Show
    (part 1)
14/05/1998 The Clip Show
    (part 2)
14/05/1998 The Finale
    (part 1)
14/05/1998 The Finale
    (part 2)

131

# Index

133